PRAISE FOR *VIEW FROM THE TOP...*

"There's an old saying I love: 'Pray like everything depends on God, but work like everything depends on you.' That could also be a great summary statement for *View From The Top*. Aaron Walker is a man who trusts God while putting a lot of sweat equity into everything he does. That balance of faith and diligence is something we all could learn from."

DAVE RAMSEY

New York Times bestselling author and
nationally syndicated radio show host

"For anyone who prefers reality over 'reality shows' that misconstrue life, Aaron Walker's *View From The Top* is as real, honest, and believable as it gets. You'll find no fluffy fiction or pious platitudes here; no 'pie in the sky.' Filled with down to earth wisdom from a successful, creative entrepreneur, Aaron openly describes both the opportunities and the pitfalls of life at the top. His contagious enthusiasm pulsates through these pages and provides hope that regardless of your past or your current circumstances, you can discover workable solutions to your everyday, real-life problems. I know that when Big A says it, I can believe it, and so can you!"

KEN ABRAHAM

New York Times bestselling author

"This terrific book by noted entrepreneur, leadership authority, and life and business coach, Aaron Walker is a powerful combination of auto-biography and success manual. If you'd like more prosperity in your business and more joy in your relationships, then dive right into this book and let Aaron help you get there!"

BOB BURG
coauthor of The Go-Giver

"Aaron Walker practices what he teaches. His desire to serve others come through on every page. He brings his life and business experiences to you in a personal way that can truly be life-changing. Read this book—and learn from the life lessons of a truly significant man!"

DAVID HANCOCK
Founder, Morgan James Publishing Company

"Success is not a destination but a mindset. This is one of many lessons I've learned from Aaron Walker. Few stories are as inspiring and challenging as this one. Get ready to embark on a journey of significance that you won't soon forget!"

JEFF GOINS
Bestselling author of The Art of Work

"In over 1,400 EOFire interviews, no guest has made a bigger impact on me or my audience, Fire Nation, than Aaron Walker. He's a shining example of how to live a life of significance. I consider him a lifelong friend."

JOHN LEE DUMAS
Entrepreneur On Fire

"Aaron's honest wisdom and desire to help others shines through in this book, and it will serve as my personal guide for living a happy and fulfilled life."

PAT FLYNN
Wall Street Journal bestselling author of *Will It Fly*
SmartPassiveIncome.com

"In *View From the Top,* Aaron Walker does more than just write about the principles of success. He shows you how to live by them, and to create a life of significance. I have the pleasure of knowing Aaron, and I can tell you he does more than teach this material; he lives it. And what's more, he teaches others how to do the same. Highly recommended!"

RAY EDWARDS
Author & Entrepreneur

"This is much more than good advice. It's deep, from the heart, and yet still practical enough to guide your actions forward. When you eventually meet Aaron Walker, you'll know this book is from his soul."

CHRIS BROGAN
CEO Owner Media Group, Inc
New York Times bestselling author of *Trust Agents*

"Aaron Walker is a man that has inspired me on many levels. When I heard his interview on The Ray Edwards Show, I refused to delete that episode until I could go back and listen to it a second time to take notes. The insights gained from that one podcast interview have helped me to have a more successful and significant life. Every time I have had a one-on-one conversation with Aaron, I come away feeling encouraged, inspired and motivated. This man is the real deal, and it's a true honor to call him a friend. I highly recommend *View from the Top*. "

CLIFF RAVENSCRAFT
CEO & Founder
PodcastAnswerMan.com

"Nobody I know lives a life of significance more than Aaron Walker. I tell my wife all the time that I want to be like Aaron when I grow up. His life proves you can be successful in business and at home. This book is a no brainer for anyone wanting to truly experience a *View from the Top* kind of life."

GRANT BALDWIN
GrantBaldwin.com

"Commitment always conquers complacency and it's the rituals and re-straints of religion that build commitment. By boldly brandishing the banner of faith in the arena of wealth creation, my dear friend and respected business professional, Aaron Walker, reveals the road map to real riches. Every page of this searingly honest book carries compelling insights which will help bring fiscal transformation to every reader."

RABBI DANIEL LAPIN

Radio & television personality and author of *Thou Shall Prosper*

"There are many rags to riches stories. What most leave out are the struggles along the way and the lessons the writer learned that you can apply. *View From The Top* is refreshingly different. Aaron Walker is an inspirational man with an amazing story. Most amazing is the authentic-ity and vulnerability he shows in sharing his life story. If you too want a *View from the Top*, read this book, study this book, and learn from the man who has been on your path and successfully found a true way to the summit in all areas of life: professional, personal, and spiritual."

TOM SCHWAB

President, Interview Valet

"Aaron Walker's *View From The Top* is like a refreshing breath of fresh air. Aaron details his journey of success with vulnerable honesty and provides a practical roadmap for anyone who would like to follow. Don't miss this one, it can be a life changer."

KEN DAVIS

International speaker, award winning comedian,
trainer of communicators

VIEW FROM
THE TOP

LIVING A LIFE OF SIGNIFICANCE

AARON WALKER

NEW YORK

NASHVILLE • MELBOURNE • VANCOUVER

VIEW FROM THE TOP

© 2017 Aaron Walker

Published in New York, New York, by Morgan James Publishing. Morgan James and The Entrepreneurial Publisher are trademarks of Morgan James, LLC. www.MorganJamesPublishing.com

The Morgan James Speakers Group can bring authors to your live event. For more information or to book an event visit The Morgan James Speakers Group at www.TheMorganJamesSpeakersGroup.com.

Shelfie

A **free** eBook edition is available with the purchase of this print book.

CLEARLY PRINT YOUR NAME ABOVE IN UPPER CASE

Instructions to claim your free eBook edition:
1. Download the Shelfie app for Android or iOS
2. Write your name in **UPPER CASE** above
3. Use the Shelfie app to submit a photo
4. Download your eBook to any device

ISBN 978-1-68350-260-9 paperback
ISBN 978-1-68350-261-6 casebound
ISBN 978-1-68350-262-3 eBook
Library of Congress Control Number:
2016915942

Cover & Interior Design by:
Megan Whitney
Creative Ninja Designs
megan@creativeninjadesigns.com

In an effort to support local communities, raise awareness and funds, Morgan James Publishing donates a percentage of all book sales for the life of each book to Habitat for Humanity Peninsula and Greater Williamsburg.

Get involved today! Visit
www.MorganJamesBuilds.com

Little did I know that at age seventeen, a chance meeting would result in the discovery of my life partner. It would be difficult to articulate the journey regardless of the allotted time. Through sleepless nights and monumental successes, I could always depend on your support. Never, not for a single moment, did I ever feel alone. Your selflessness, devotion, and unyielding inspiration have always been my catalyst.

To my beautiful and loving wife Robin: it's all because of you.

TABLE OF CONTENTS

Foreword xv

Note to Reader xix

CHAPTER 1   Can't Couldn't Do It, and Could Did It All 1

CHAPTER 2   Immeasurable Rewards Are Headed Your Way 19

CHAPTER 3   Finished at Twenty-Seven 31

CHAPTER 4   Breaking Free 45

CHAPTER 5   Setting Boundaries 61

CHAPTER 6   Blindsided 69

CHAPTER 7   The Eagles 85

CHAPTER 8   Iron Sharpens Iron 99

CHAPTER 9   Focus 109

CHAPTER 10   Choose Wisely 123

CHAPTER 11   Retire! What Is That? 131

CHAPTER 12   Can You Handle the Truth? .143

CHAPTER 13   Bitterness Is Its Own Prison 157

CHAPTER 14   Put the Big Rocks in First 165

CHAPTER 15   An Indescribable View 179

Next Step 191

Living the Transformed Life 193

About the Author 197

FOREWORD

When I was just thirteen years old my life was dramatically impacted by a little recording called *The Strangest Secret*. The message presented was essentially the Biblical principle— "As a man thinketh in his heart, so is he." I learned the power of feeding my mind positive, faith-building thoughts as opposed to allowing the challenges of a legalistic religion and a poor farm life to determine my attitude and future. And I learned that by taking responsibility for my thinking I could determine the direction of my life. I discovered we can all choose to tell our life story as a victim or as someone who has chosen to walk in victory and abundance.

In this very hopeful and inspiring book Aaron shares his own story of early poverty, family heartache, and misfortune—and how those experiences could have left him trapped in anger, fear and having little. But his continued search for answers and solutions also led to his discovery that he was not trapped or limited—he had a choice. He could move beyond those limitations to be more successful more quickly than family and peers. With a creative approach he began his first entrepreneurial business at age eleven, accelerated his high school obligations, moved fully into business, and then was able to retire a wealthy "man" at age twenty-seven.

Those early successes forced Aaron to take a fresh look at what success really meant. Perhaps it's not just sitting on the front porch or playing golf every day. What if success means having something meaningful and productive to do each day?

We all dream of and wish for lives of happiness, meaning, and fulfillment. And yet, it seems that reality assures us that we will experience hardships along the way. God has apparently designed us to grow from the unexpected struggles that inevitably show up. But like the butterfly struggling to get out of the cocoon, our struggles are part of what makes us fully alive. And like the butterfly, those struggles are not intended to limit or cripple us, but to allow us to develop our resilience, fortitude, compassion, and personal excellence. Fifteen years ago Aaron had a life-changing experience that caused him to look at life through a new lens. While business may be great, a larger question is what kind of legacy are we creating? How will people remember us when we're gone?

In the award winning movie *The King's Speech,* the Duke of York was thrust into the role of king when unexpectedly he was crowned King George IV. He was challenged to "have faith in his voice" while dealing with a debilitating stammer. That faith was about much more than just pushing words out of his mouth. He had to believe he had a message worth sharing to find his voice. In that gut-wrenching but thrilling process the Duke found his voice, thus becoming confident and able to galvanize his countrymen for uncommon greatness.

Aaron describes his own process for finding what for him was an unexpected "voice." And he describes the process by which we can all make the choices for finding our unique voice—even when circumstances seem to make us stammer. *View from the Top* gently guides us through the process of recognizing our greatest God-given talents. Of using our hearts and heads even if we are most familiar with the work of our hands. Of stretching in areas that culture and tradition have warned us against. Of acting in our passion even when others say that's unrealistic and impractical. Aaron helps us understand what Maya Angelo meant in saying, "When you know better, you do better." This is a book to help us know, and do, better. Integrity, character, and daily growth can lead us to new adventures—new work, new successes, and new ways to make a positive impact. In a volatile workplace our daily work can change dramatically, requiring us to use new technologies and unfamiliar methods that we may not have felt prepared for.

I challenge you to open your heart and discover how the unexplained and often unwelcomed events in our lives can move us toward the greatness intended for each of us. As we move away from our own insecurities and fears, we release the best in ourselves and encourage the same in those around us.

You are doing something special for others and yourself—by reading *View from the Top!* The investment of your time will come back multiplied with more confidence and enthusiasm—and you'll discover your own powerful voice that will inspire and encourage others along the way.

DAN MILLER
Author and Life Coach
www.48Days.com

NOTE TO READER

Welcome to *View from the Top*.

Life's a journey, not a destination. I'm sure you've heard this before, but have you ever wondered how some people's journeys lead them to seemingly unlimited success, and others rarely experience success at all?

The outcome of your journey or mine is yet to be determined. The mere fact that you are reading this book is evidence of your quest to learn and implement new tactics and strategies. Regardless of where you are, there's more to be done.

My name is Aaron Walker, but my friends and family call me Big A. I have written *View from the Top* to share with you parts of my personal journey towards success and significance. Financially, my journey started from humble beginnings. My parents were deeply committed and had character traits above reproach; we just didn't have much money. Along the way, God has blessed me beyond my wildest expectations.

In the following pages, you will witness a life of unexpected twists and turns. I have experienced unbelievable successes early in my adult life coupled with many sleepless nights. My desire is that you will find hope and inspiration and glean insights from the lessons I have learned along the way. I honestly believe that if you will learn at my expense (and it's always better to learn at someone else's expense) that you too can have an incredible view that maybe up until this point has only been a dream.

In sharing my life experiences, I have been completely raw and transparent. Success is never a direct forward incline void of trials. There will be pitfalls. In my story I describe some troubling ones that have ensnared me over the years. I also offer possible solutions that may enable you to avoid them. That's what I mean by learning at my expense—avoiding problems by taking someone's advice who has been through it.

Have you ever noticed that you "lean in" when you're interested in a subject to capture every detail? Whenever you are excited, intrigued, impressed, or inspired by someone else's words, you naturally find yourself on the edge of your seat, making sure that you don't miss any part of the conversation. I have taken the time to draw out what I feel to be vitally relevant in each chapter and restated these key points in a section titled "Lean In." Use this section as a quick reference for a moment of reflection and inspiration.

I have also created some resources to assist you on your journey. Feel free to refer back to them as often as needed while you read this book. I want to make this journey as easy as possible for you. Simply go to the following page: www.ViewFromTheTop.com/leanin

Early on, my total focus was centered on achieving huge success. I was mesmerized by the glitz and glamour. After sampling only a small taste, I realized there had to be more. There was a void that was indescribable. Over time, I found the piece that was missing was significance, and how I discovered that was not fun. My primary objective is for you to be able to learn from my journey so you can have your view from the top.

I guess you could settle for average, being just as close to the bottom as you are to the top. Or, you could be proactive and build a life that is second to none. It's your choice, and only you can choose.

Are you ready? Let's get started.

CHAPTER 1

CAN'T COULDN'T DO IT, AND COULD DID IT ALL

We live in a time that is unlike any other in history. With all the advances in technology and the accessibility to information, we've become a society that has been overwhelmed by the plague of instant gratification. It's easy today to get frustrated because we don't succeed fast enough or we don't see the results of our efforts quickly enough. People tend to get frustrated more easily and quit before they've really given themselves a chance to succeed.

Success is not for the faint of heart. It's not going to be handed to you; the universe will not simply bestow it upon you, and your ship is not going to come in without someone at the helm to pilot it safely to shore. To be successful, all of us must answer some very important questions: Is it possible? Can I do it? Do I have the wherewithal buried deep inside me to be a winner? *I feel there is a champion inside of me, but fear lies just below the surface.* Is it remotely possible to be successful in this life, even if you are starting from scratch? When there is no privileged background or even a hint of resources, is it worth the effort?

Many people go through life thinking that success is only available to those who are born into it. They get trapped in the mindset that because they grew up a certain way or because of things that happened in their past, success is just not in their future. I can tell you from my personal experience, that's just not true. It doesn't matter *where* you start, what is important is *that* you start. This book was written so I could share my journey to significance with you.

I've had my ups and downs and have been through good times, bad times, and times that land somewhere in the middle. I started from humble beginnings and now enjoy my view from the top, but it didn't happen overnight. It took a journey for me to get where I am today, and it will take a journey of your own to get you to the life you want to live.

I hope you will learn from my story and take these principles, which have allowed me to succeed, and create your own journey that leads you to your very own view from the top.

Hello, my name is Aaron Walker, and this is my story . . .

I grew up in a quaint suburb ten miles north of Nashville, called Madison, Tennessee. We lived in an area called Neely's Bend. It was a seven-mile stretch of land surrounded on three sides, sort of a peninsula, by the Cumberland River.

My dad, Johnny Walker, was a carpenter. His small home building company was appropriately named Walker Home Builders. This was a very small operation, focusing on single projects, and small ones at that.

My mom, Lucy, was a part-time church secretary and full-time mom, juggling multiple balls, trying to make ends meet. I'm privileged to have one older brother, Steven, an older sister, Julie, and a younger brother, Michael. I guess you figured it out; I am number three in the pecking order.

The 60s were difficult years, and it was particularly challenging at the Walker's. By the time I was six or seven years old, my dad fell on hard times. Needless to say, he didn't handle that well. Unfortunately, bad habits were lurking in the shadows—alcohol. I realize his stress levels at this time must have been unbearable, and I'm sorry to report, my dad gave in to the numbing effect that alcohol provides. It was a very uncomfortable and strange time in my life. I was young, and this state of confusion was new to my family. Whispering in the background, private, closed-door meetings, and a room full of tension had not been the norm. I remember times in the car when I was unsure of my dad's ability to drive. Normally, my dad's jovial personality was the center of attention, but strife and anger took its place.

Over the course of a lifetime, we experience trials and tribulations, but 1968 is a year to be forgotten, if at all possible. That was the year that our family suffered financial ruin. At the time, I was sheltered, as I should have been; my parents were very protective. I can only begin to imagine what my mom and dad were feeling. The Walkers are very prideful, right or wrong, but banks are very unforgiving, especially when you are not paying the mortgage. Our tiny house (today, that's in vogue) was soon to be a memory.

Our relatives, only a couple of miles away, invited us to move in while we looked for a new place. My mom was such an encourager to my dad and all the kids; she assured everyone that we would be okay. All the while, my parents' relationship was rocky at best. My dad was very independent and didn't spend much time seeking advice from others. He could have benefited greatly from a trusted friend with good advice, but he was very private and did not want others to know about his personal business—or the lack of it.

Even though I was not fully aware, and honestly didn't know to care at the time, I remember the sadness. Laughter was noticeably absent. I knew something was wrong; I just didn't know what it was.

Experiencing these kinds of trials will certainly have an impact on the way you view life—many times negatively—but I honestly feel that this experience instilled grit deep into my being. I feel as though perseverance and determination were ingrained into the very fiber of my soul. Thank you, Lord, for uninvited bankruptcy.

Going through this and experiencing it with my family taught me how to fight. It showed me that I could survive and that knowledge instilled in me the tools to survive and later excel.

Patience is a virtue that few have. I'm confident that I would have been much less patient had I not gone through these trials as a child. My mom taught us early on that you can't have everything you want immediately. This has proven to be a treasured tool and life lesson. Born out of patience was creativity. Now, I have the ability to look at projects and opportunities in multidimensional phases. Sometimes, unexpected force causes great creativity. So even through great struggle, there can be significant benefit.

I knew the day of reckoning was near. I could feel the days were numbered, and my mom's tipping point was at hand. She finally gave my dad the ultimatum. She said, "You can stop drinking and do what's right, or you're going to lose your family." Thankfully, my dad elected to do the right thing; he quit drinking and got his head back in the game. Thank goodness he made the right choice. So many don't, and the negative impact is felt for generations. I don't know how my life would have changed if he had made a different choice, but I suspect it would have been much more challenging.

My dad passed away in 2006, and I have to say that he was, without question, my best friend. The character traits and work habits that he taught me are, to this day, invaluable. He said, "Son, if somebody is going to pay you to do a job, you have to be willing to give all you've got."

You have to set the standards by which you measure how well you do the things you do, but you should always be willing to give more than what's expected. The view from the top is reserved for those who do just a little bit more. It's never good to do just enough to squeak by; average people can do that. Always remember, you are far and above average. If you want to have more, you have to do more. I learned early on to give above the minimal requirements.

Always remember, you are far and above average. If you want to have more, you have to do more.

My dad taught me a lot of valuable lessons as a child; character was a big deal to Dad. If you gave your word, he would see to it that you followed through. Many times the truth would lead to punishment, but the severity of the discipline was much greater if it came about as the result of a lie. Respect was another trait that my dad demanded and modeled. Despite all the valuable attributes that my father was gifted with, there was one much-needed quality he did not have. My dad was a horrible businessman. He was risk averse, and his education was limited. He had male pride that was larger than life. He always wanted to be in charge, and he was. He felt it was shameful to ask for help; it showed a sign of weakness. This is where things went awry. Dad would do things the hard way just to show it could be done. For him, it was always brute strength and force where necessary. If a little is good, more must be better was his motto.

We used to tease around our house about hanging pictures or fixing anything. Dad would always use three times more supplies (whether it was nails, tape, glue, etc.) than what was needed to complete the task. We would say, "You Johnny Walkered that, didn't you?" As I was growing up, I often wondered, *With such limited experience in business, why would Dad want to be self-employed?* The truth is, he didn't wish to work for somebody else, but he wouldn't take the initiative to learn the business fundamentals and principles he needed to run a successful business himself.

He didn't want to ask anybody for help. He never wanted you to think he didn't know something. As I said earlier, he had a lot of great attributes, like character and integrity—he was honest to a fault—but he was very, very prideful, and that was a stumbling block for him. Through my dad's struggles, I saw early on the benefit of getting help. You just have to be willing to set your pride and ego aside for the greater benefits.

Asking for help doesn't make you any less of a person. It's much better to be transparent, let your veil down, and show people that you need help. It's not a sign of weakness; it's a sign of strength. I learned early on to ask a lot of questions, and even today, I still do. You don't know what you don't know. I don't mind asking about the things I don't understand. Asking questions does not show a lack of ability; it shows your willingness to let your pride go and not let it get in the way of your progress and ultimate success.

I will discuss this a little later, but for now, I will just say that you need trusted advisors who are unbiased. You need people in your corner, cheering you on. Many times we desire that voice of reason or that word of caution. During rough spots throughout our journey, we count on others we can reach out to and get that much-sought-after advice to move forward. When things get rough, and they will, close friends and meaningful relationships are crucial.

A valuable lesson I learned from my dad was what I *didn't* want to do in life. I did not want to work as hard, physically, as my dad did his entire career. I witnessed firsthand the abuse his body endured. I remember the days and weeks he spent at home in the bed as a result of an electrical shock; I remember his bruised and battered body from manhandling construction material. Being self-employed had its perks, along with its disadvantages. There is no question that the toll his body endured for fifty-plus years was devastating. Each season of the year brought new challenges: heat in the summer and frostbite in the winter. Watching Dad sweep snow off a roof so that he could repair it or hand dig a water line gave me two distinctly different opinions. First, I gained a whole new appreciation for my dad and his willingness to do whatever he needed to to provide for us. My dad was a man's man and loved his family. Second, it instilled deep in my inner self a desire to do life differently. I could tell that Dad stayed in a lot of physical pain the majority of his life, and for that, I will always feel a sense of indebtedness.

> You have to be deliberate, intentional, and action-oriented.

Now, I don't mind working hard, and I believe grit, determination, and perseverance are cornerstones of success. You've got to be relentless; you have to put in your time. It's called the ten thousand-hour rule. To be proficient or to be considered great requires an inordinate amount of diligence. You have to be deliberate, intentional, and action-oriented. You've got to put in the hard work, and my dad was doing that, based on what he knew. He would have had much greater success had he been able to surround himself with qualified and competent professionals. These experts will never come to you offering assistance. You must be proactive in education and always take the initiative to learn more.

I used these lessons early on in my life. When I was ten years old, I got one of my first jobs at a little store called The Bread Box, across the street from my school. I used to go to work in the afternoon, stocking shelves, straightening up, and sweeping the floors. Whatever was needed in that little community store, I was willing to do.

I was not content with an afternoon job. Saturdays offered up a better opportunity to make money than any other day. Jessie Cole, our next-door neighbor, owned a home meat delivery service. I volunteered, for minimal hourly pay, to work alongside Mr. Cole. I would help him by stocking the cooler, getting the meat out, and delivering it. I started working young, but I just enjoyed the process—as well as the money. My mom and dad didn't have much disposable income, and neither of them believed in allowances. So, the rational thing to me was, if you want to buy things, you've got to have a job.

When I turned eleven years old, the entrepreneurial bug hit. The afternoon job at the local market and my Saturday meat business primed the financial pump. My mom worked as a secretary at our local church. I heard about an opportunity to cut the church lawn, and I quickly asked for permission to bid. I think my mom was the inside track that landed the contract. I got tired fast using a push mower; it was a huge yard, especially to someone eleven years old. I saved my money, went down to the local Western Auto, and bought a brand new, yellow Wizard riding lawnmower. I paid just over three hundred dollars, and that was like buying a house to me at the time. I'm not sure what that equates to now, but when you are eleven, it's a lot. I guess you could say this was my first lesson in investing in my business growth. The riding mower allowed me to cut grass faster and more easily, which meant I could cut more yards. I started to cut my next-door neighbor's yard. Then I started cutting his next-door neighbor's yard, and then I started cutting our yard, and eventually I had a route that I did each week. I ended up making pretty good money.

I had parents who taught, if you want something, then get busy figuring out a way to get it. They taught me how to do and think on my own. I knew that no one else was going to do the hard lifting for me, and if I wanted a better life, I had to do it myself. Although I always had the support and encouragement of my parents, they believed in that ancient proverb of teaching someone to fish rather than giving him the fish.

If you spend your life waiting for someone else to bring success to you, then you'll be waiting a long time. Entitlement at my house was as extinct as a prehistoric dinosaur. You are not entitled to success any more than you have a right to anything. You have the right to pursue success, and it's in the pursuit that you can find your meaning and purpose.

When I turned thirteen years old, my dad asked me if I wanted to help him remodel a health club and turn it into a pawnshop. I was all in if I could make some money. It took about three months to convert this health studio into a pawnshop. I'll never forget it. Herb Berry owned the store and was twenty-three years old at the time. His family had been in the pawn business in Nashville since 1941, and he had chosen Madison to open up a store of his own after he graduated college.

I seriously don't know why, but I had the courage to approach Herb and ask him for a job. I had only met him a couple of times, but I liked him. We were finishing up construction and leaving that August day in 1974 when it just happened to dawn on me that this could be an awesome opportunity. I told him that I would do whatever he needed every day, including cleaning and stock work if he would consider hiring me.

He hired me on the spot. This was the shortest interview in history. He told me that anybody with this much initiative would have to be an exceptional employee, and he said, "Welcome aboard."

People were bringing jewelry, tools, and guns into the pawnshop daily; they were leaving the items, and we were giving them money. I had never seen a pawnshop before, so I didn't understand what was happening. After about two weeks, I asked Herb what these people were doing. I said, "They're bringing in all their stuff, and you're giving them money; are you buying it?" He told me we were loaning them money. They had three months to come back and get it, or we were going to sell it. That was very intriguing to me. I quickly fell in love with this business and started to enjoy the diversity of the people.

By the time I was fifteen years old, I knew that I wanted to own my own business. I enjoyed working; I enjoyed the relationships that I was building; I enjoyed making money. But, more importantly, I enjoyed the freedom and accomplishment I felt.

While most of the guys my age were involved in sports or were just enjoying their high school years, I was working. I wanted success in a different kind of way than I had experienced up to this point. There was not one thing wrong with how my mom and dad raised me; as a matter of fact, they had done a remarkable job. I just wanted to see a little more of the world. I knew the only way I was going to get there was to do the hard work and the heavy lifting. So that's exactly what I did.

I knew that in order to be good at any one thing, it takes total commitment and a sense of devotion, and I was willing to do that. Sports were not as important to me as living a fulfilled and complete life. I wanted nice things; I wanted to travel and see parts of the world that I had never experienced as of yet.

In life, you must make choices. You can't have "everything" at one time. You need to focus on what is important to you long-term, and for me, that was creating a financially secure life so that later I could enjoy many great experiences, rather than just the immediate pleasures of life.

One of the most important disciplines you can have in life is the ability to delay gratification. Focus on the things that are really important long-term so you can enjoy those benefits when it's time. Even now, as a businessman, there are only a handful of things that I'll do, but I will do those things to the best of my ability, weighing all the cost for the betterment of everyone involved.

"Be an inch wide and a mile deep." This is a great saying by Greg McKeown, the author of *Essentialism*. I believe you should be exceptional at everything you attempt. You have to decide what's important to you. We don't have the bandwidth to do all things, but those items you select need your focus, and you must give them 100 percent and attempt to be second to none. Set your sights on the prize and don't waiver.

I wanted to succeed badly enough that all I could think about were ways to get out of school faster so I could get to work earlier. A friend of mine in high school sat in front of me during second period. I told her I had to get out of school as soon as possible. She asked what I meant. I said, "I want to work; I don't want to go to school any longer than necessary." She explained that her brother had entered a co-op program, and if I went to talk to them in the guidance office, there might be a way to speed up the process for me as well.

The counselors graciously explained to me about a program that Watkins Institute had for unusual circumstances. It was a magnet school where students could go to earn the credits needed to graduate high school, and they could be earned over the summer and in the evenings.

I started summer school right away. I would go for half a day to Watkins Institute, and I'd go to work. Then I'd leave work and go to night school. I did that for about eighteen months. By the time I started my junior year in high school, I had enough credits to graduate. I only had to attend one class my junior year, and I'd get there at eight o'clock every morning, and I'd be out at half past nine. After that, I would go straight to Berry's Pawn. My senior year, I only had to show up twice; I registered in early September, and I graduated mid-June. I spent two hours in school my last year; pretty sweet, huh? This allowed me to work every day, all day long.

It didn't take very long before I began to think about what it would be like to become the owner of a pawnshop. I knew I was young, but I was ambitious and believed I could do anything I set my mind to. My mom taught me a saying when I was young that has empowered me to move continually forward. She would say, "Can't couldn't do it, and could did it all." This has become my life mantra.

You have to have a can-do attitude in anything you want to excel at. Remove "can't" from your vocabulary and figure out a way to do the things you want. When asked if I can do something, my reply is, "Yes, just give me a little time to figure it out." Remember, while it may not be perfect at first, you'll be surprised at what you can do with proper instruction and a little time. Can you? Absolutely!

People often allow themselves to believe they have to do it all alone and that's the only way to get started. I say, "Bull. It's not. Who wrote that script? You can do anything you want if you want it badly enough." There are no rules when it comes to who you work with or how you get started. If you want to do something badly enough, you will figure out a way, and you won't allow anything to get in your way—even if that means asking someone else for help.

Around this time, I also knew two guys named Roger Street and Dale Garrett. They were in the insurance business and were extremely successful, but they were looking for different ways to protect their money as they felt a certain percentage of their wealth should be diversified. Diamonds and gold seemed like a natural fit, so they were buying diamonds and gold from me to hedge against inflation.

I knew they had money because of the amount and types of deals they were making with the pawnshop. One day, I asked them if they had ever had any interest in going into the pawnshop business. They laughed initially and then asked how old I was. "Eighteen," I proudly announced. They were shocked because someone so young had never approached them, asking to go into business. I told them that I had been in the pawn business for five years now, and I knew the business very well. I just got an early start.

They thought about it and called me back after a couple of weeks. They asked me to come by their office, which was nearby, and I met with them. They asked me how much it would cost to start a pawnshop. I'm embarrassed to admit that, at that time, I didn't have a clue, but I told them I'd find out and get back to them soon. Over the next two weeks, I did as much homework as I knew how to do. I had never put together a business plan or a pro forma of any kind. I did as much research as possible, and I figured that it would take $150,000. I'll be the first to say that, in 1979, that was a lot of money. Before I made any final decisions with Roger and Dale, I went to Herb Berry and asked him if I'd ever have an opportunity to own part of his business. He said, "Absolutely not." Berry told me that it was a family business, and they had no intentions of selling. He was very gracious, but convincing.

No, to me, just means no for the day; it doesn't mean no forever. No means no until you figure a way to make it a yes. Most people would have stopped at that point. They'd say, "I got a no; that was my one and only shot." Sorry, but that's not the way I think! No is often temporary. It means no for this conversation. Herb was a great guy, but I had to fend for myself and strive towards the dreams and goals I had created. Roger and Dale were available for a wonderful business opportunity, and I did not want to waste this chance. What if they said no? I guess I would have found somebody else to explore the possibilities with. You have to make your way. Where there is no trail, make one.

Where there is no trail, make one.

To my surprise, I was being investigated. Being astute businessmen, Roger and Dale were conducting their background check on me. Community leaders, church personnel, and school teachers were all being contacted regarding my abilities and character. If I had known this, I would have been nervous, to say the least. This was another life and business lesson to me regarding due diligence. They were checking on me to make sure I was an upstanding guy who possessed the needed skills to be their partner. When they were satisfied with the results of their search, they said they were going to do the deal with me. I was elated and scared to death all at the same time. They insisted we borrow the $150,000, and all three of us were co-signers. I did not care because I had nothing to lose. They had the money, but they wanted me to be responsible for the money as well.

I'll never forget that day. I walked out of the bank with a grand vision and a checkbook with a $150,000 balance. Roger and Dale said, "Well, go open the pawnshop." I got in my car and instantly felt like I was going to throw up. I was a nervous wreck, and I remember my only thought: *Lord, we have to do this; I need your help.*

Just because you do your homework and have a plan in place doesn't mean that you know what to do. We all know that experience is the best teacher, and I had an employee background, but no experience as an owner. When you put yourself in a position of leadership, you have to lead. I look at failure a little differently than most. You either succeed or you learn. I was prepared for either. There were a lot of things I didn't know when I started my first pawnshop, and there will be a lot of stuff you won't know as you start your journey to your view from the top. That doesn't mean that you stop or delay your start; it just means you do what you can with the information available.

The first thing I did was look for a location for my store. I found a shopping center in East Nashville called the Crescent Plaza Shopping Center. It was owned by Charlie Wheeler, a very successful real estate investor, so I called him and voiced an interest in the available space. I had never negotiated a lease before; I had no clue what I was doing. But I did as much research as I could, and he never knew the difference. At least, that is what I convinced myself to believe. I consummated the lease and took possession of our first location.

I visited yard sales, flea markets, and any other places I could think of that sold used merchandise. I bought everything and anything I thought I had a decent shot at selling. As I was preparing the store to open, I brought my purchases in, cleaned them up, and displayed them like I had done for years at Berry's. This was the most difficult part of the inventory selection because everything was used; it was more difficult to find quality merchandise that I was proud to offer. Buying new jewelry was easy; there were countless suppliers.

Our grand opening was May 28, 1979. Aaron's Jewelry & Loan Co. was open for business. We hired a local band and had a huge opening. Sales were awesome; we had been promoting the event for weeks. However, the first loan I made was for thirty dollars. It was a pair of ruby earrings with a matching necklace. My very first loan wound up being on stolen jewelry. What a way to start a new business! I remember thinking, *I hope this isn't a sign of bad things to come.* Fortunately, it was a fluke.

Robin and I were dating at the time; she was still in high school but more than willing to help me in the afternoons and evenings. I could not afford an employee, so I worked there alone for the first eighteen months. At night, we would go out and put flyers on car windshields or in mailboxes. The post office would call and tell me that it was against the law to put flyers in mailboxes. They told me I would need to come and pick all the flyers up. Well, I'd go and do it again the next evening. I didn't have much regard for that kind of law at the time. All I could think about was that $150,000 loan I was responsible for. I thought it was ridiculous to have a perfectly good mailbox that I was not allowed to put a flyer in. Finally, they gave me a very stern and final warning. The United States Postal Service explained to me in plain English what the future consequences were if I repeated the offence.

I started going to all the shopping centers and putting my flyers on the windshields of cars. Again, my back was against the wall. Kroger complained that hundreds of advertisements were littering their parking lot. I continued relentlessly until legal action was threatened. Remember my philosophy: no is temporary. I had to come up with a different method or strategy. We started taping the flyers to the mailboxes in the afternoon or knocking on the doors and meeting people. It was illegal to put something *in* the mailbox but nothing prohibited placing a flyer *on* the mailbox. I'll be honest with you; it was grueling. I was so tired every night that we did that. Day in, day out, we walked the streets and distributed flyers, relentlessly trying to grow our business. Well, God honored

Quit taking no as the answer and find a way.

our efforts, and people from every area of the community started coming in. They started taking loans, and the business grew exponentially.

Doing the hard task is what makes us successful. If success were easy, then everybody would be successful. But it's not easy, and often, it's not fun either. Many people are not willing to do what's necessary to get ahead in life; it's easier to stay where you are than it is to cut through the obstacles and get to higher ground.

There's always a way—if you want to do it. Quit taking no as the answer and find a way. It may not be easy, but it will be worth it. Believe me, going to summer and night school and working full time was not fun. It wasn't easy, and at times, I wanted to quit. I didn't go to parties; I elected not to play sports; and I didn't go out a lot when I was in school. I studied; I went to work during the day; and I went to school at night. That was hard work. But as a result of those efforts, today I can do things that I want to do because I was willing to focus on long-term success and delay immediate gratification. Everything described here can be duplicated by you. There were no exceptional opportunities, just a plan and execution.

LEAN IN . . .

- You have to set the standards by which you measure how well you do the things you do, but you should always be willing to give more than what's expected. The view from the top is reserved for those who do just a little bit more.

- Grit, determination, and perseverance are cornerstones of success. You've got to be relentless; you have to put in your time.

- One of the most important disciplines you can have in life is the ability to delay gratification. Focus on the things that are really important long-term so you can enjoy those benefits when it's time.

- Remove "can't" from your vocabulary and figure out a way to do the things you want.

- Many people are not willing to do what's necessary to get ahead in life; it's easier to stay where you are than it is to cut through the obstacles and get to higher ground.

CHAPTER 2

IMMEASURABLE REWARDS ARE HEADED YOUR WAY

A very common stumbling block today is the desire for instant gratification. Many are looking for opportunities that bring fast cash, immediate results, or continuous pleasure. This is exactly why the fad diet business is one of the most lucrative industries in the world to be involved with.

Consumers buy into the hype of "lose weight now with minimal or no effort!" Sophisticated advertisers play on our emotions and suggest that "even *you* can have dramatic results instantly with this recently discovered program." Without warning, our inner desire to once again be fit and trim overrides logic and says, *Give it a try. What have you got to lose?*

I'm not saying there's anything wrong with quick results or immediate progress. In fact, I like fast action and even faster success, but there are risks with living a life of instant gratification. More often than not, we overlook the details that could suggest different outcomes in our race towards success. Having a predetermined due diligence time frame for most significant decisions will pay off handsomely.

One thing we know is that most fad diets fail. Either people don't really see the full benefit that was promised in the ad, or if they do, they don't keep the weight off. They often find themselves right back in the same situation they were in before they started the program (and usually heavier than they were before starting it).

Take a moment and step outside of yourself. Take a thirty-thousand-foot hypothetical view, if you can. Visualize a time line that is representative of your lifetime. From birth until death, normally speaking, is seventy-five to eighty years. That's a long time. You need to have quick wins on a regular basis, but the majority of our time should be spent on long-term goals that bring you to a bigger and better place in life. It's okay to have quick victories and fast results as long as they lead to a larger vision and move you toward the life you want to live.

> It's okay to have quick victories and fast results as long as they lead to a larger vision and move you toward the life you want to live.

There is no question in my mind that if you'll put the time, effort, and energy into a focused vision for your future, you will see those short, quick wins, all while working on the grander plan. But when you have sustained wins, the long-term benefits of doing something over an extended period of time, the rewards you'll receive will be immeasurable. I've always attempted to live my life with the end goal in mind.

Two weeks after Robin graduated from high school, we got married. I was nineteen; she was barely eighteen. I had been working daily by myself for just over a year. Looking back, this was very dangerous. I was the founder, salesman, stock boy, and janitor all rolled neatly into a single package. Hey, when you are just getting started, you have to do whatever it takes to make it. Robin would come and help me at the store in the evenings until our business grew enough that I was able to hire somebody. As a side note for all those start-ups, be very mindful of your expenses when you begin. Most companies fail within the first two years as a direct result of being undercapitalized. A good way to offset this dilemma is to be mindful of your expenses. Don't sacrifice growth, just grow when you can really afford it.

Robin and I decided to run our business in the same manner I'd lived my life to that point. We didn't go out and mortgage ourselves to the hilt; we didn't get the fancy, big car right out of the gate just because we were making a little bit of money. Instead, we decided to put our money back into the business. We wanted to grow something that would support our dreams in the future.

We were very ambitious and full of excitement and enthusiasm. We both came from very humble origins, and we did not want to waste this opportunity. We discussed at length the limited experience that either of us had and decided we should move very deliberately, with great caution. Looking back, I see now that time was in our favor, but when you are in the moment, you feel as though you have to make a hasty decision. You don't! A lifetime is a really long time; slow down and make excellent choices.

This is where most people get tripped up. They believe the old myth that life is short. Living with that mindset makes it too easy to blow money and waste opportunities to build a secure future. You have to ask yourself, *Do I want to enjoy my success right now, or do I want to enjoy my success forever?*

We figured out pretty early how to delay gratification for long-term gain. At the time, I didn't say, "We are going to delay gratification." I didn't really even know that term. What I knew was that the sooner we removed the debt, the sooner I could sleep again and get that knot out of my stomach. Today, I would say we delayed gratification. I will say that everything we did in business, we did with the future in mind.

I would have loved to increase my lifestyle in those early days, but instead, we chose to reinvest into other stores and outside real estate investments. Looking back now, I can say that it has paid huge dividends. One of the real estate investments we made over twenty-five years ago was a commercial building. The Fortune 500 company that bought my business has been the tenant since 1989. Doing something strategic, not necessarily genius, has the ability, over time, to pay residual income into perpetuity. As a result of the long-term investment, we are able to sit back and enjoy the benefits now. I would encourage you to be open-minded when looking at solid investments. The sooner you get started, the sooner you will reap the benefits. Don't do something that would jeopardize the safety of your family, but don't be so conservative that you miss great opportunities.

That's the way you have to look at a business: long-term. Yes, you could live like a flamboyant executive, drive a BMW, visit the Caribbean biannually, and have a house that is the envy of the community. However, what if a few brilliant business decisions turn south? What if that "big deal" falls through? What if the economy takes a dip, and you wake up one morning to hear on Fox News that your stock portfolio took a bath overnight? Now what? When you over-extend and are leveraged to the max, you may just be playing with fire. Take calculated risks while protecting your family from inherent danger. Move slowly while investing wisely. You signed up to provide for and protect your family. It's incumbent on you to do just that.

I lived through my dad's bankruptcy early on in my life. I was a child, and I don't remember much about it other than bouncing around for a few months until we were re-established. We were casualties of a rough economy in the late 60s. Even so, there are repercussions that will forever be burned into my memory. One day all was great, and like a thief in the night, it was gone.

I'm pretty confident that you want financial security; who wouldn't? But be very careful placing your confidence and security in tangible possessions. When too much emphasis is placed on stuff, you are sure to be disappointed. I want you to enjoy the things you have; just don't make them your central focus.

There are endless experiences before us. I remember studying geography in school and daydreaming often about what it might be like to visit these locations in person. Quickly, I came to my senses and reality set in. After all, it's very expensive to travel. I wanted to experience all those places, but that takes an inordinate amount of resources. If I truly wanted to explore the possibility of visiting other countries, it would be necessary for me to work tirelessly, invest wisely, and forgo many of the ordinary conveniences. So, here we are again with a decision. Do I attempt to have everything, or do I focus on the few, vital things I really want? Thankfully, we focused intently on a few things and were frugal with what we had been entrusted with. Now we have the privilege of traveling and seeing a lot of the world and experiencing what it has to offer—all because we delayed gratification until the appropriate time.

Delaying gratification is one of the most difficult things you will ever do; it's also one of the most rewarding things you can do. As hard as it is, though, it may not be the hardest part of your journey. The hardest part for most people is asking for help.

I've needed help many times in my life, and I continue to need others' assistance today. I understand asking for help is admitting there is a lack of ability on my part, and I'm okay with that. There are certain areas of our life where we are very skilled, and there are other areas in which we need help. I would encourage you to be okay with admitting to those areas you need help with. You don't know what you don't know, and you don't have what you don't have, and you never will either—unless you ask for that much-needed help.

Why wouldn't you want to get the help you need? Are you embarrassed to ask? It's more embarrassing to admit you failed because your pride got in the way. Your ego will take you places you don't want to go and keep you longer than you wanted to stay. When people ask you what happened or why you failed, do you really want to answer them with, "I was afraid to ask for help"?

If you find it difficult asking other people for assistance, you're not alone. Many have a hard time asking for help because they are afraid of being rejected or they don't want to feel like a burden to someone else. Fear of rejection is at the top of the list as to why people won't ask someone else to help them. Please allow me to share the truth about asking for help. Lean in, and listen carefully. When you are honest with those who care about you and are vulnerable and transparent, revealing your weaknesses in a tactful manner, you just arrived at the intersection where strength begins.

You've got to get over that fear of rejection. I faced this when I was a teenager, as an eighteen-year-old kid who wanted to start a pawnshop but needed money that I didn't have. It was very apparent that if this venture happened, I was going to need a venture capitalist or a partner. I chose the latter. I approached two local Nashvillians who owned the twenty-first largest insurance agency in the country at the time. Was I nervous? There was not a bone in my body that was not shivering at the thought of what they might say. As I thought through the situation, I began to ask myself, *What's the worst thing that could happen?* They could say no. Well, if I hadn't asked them, the answer would have absolutely been no!

I went to two successful entrepreneurs to get the money because they had it. I knew I needed resources and business experience, and these two guys had both. I would have never gotten the money, and the dream of having my own business would have never been realized, if I didn't ask them for help. I asked for help, got the money I needed, and started my first business. If you ever want your own view from the top, at some point, you will have to be willing to swallow your pride, muster up the courage, and ask for help when you need it.

It's a sad irony that during the times people most need to ask for help, so many are hesitant in doing so. There are folks out there today who have the resources you need, and all you have to do is ask. Recently a friend of mine got a very notable endorsement for his new book. I was in awe when he shared with me this huge victory. I'll have to admit; just for a second, I was a little envious. How awesome it must have felt for him to get such a powerful figure to acknowledge his work. My curiosity finally got the best of me, and I asked how

> If your dreams are important enough, you will find a way to make them happen.

he landed such a prized catch. He said, "I asked." People are not getting the help they need because they are not asking for it. I have many friends and colleagues who are flush with cash, but they can't find dedicated and capable people to do business with.

There's more money on the sidelines right now than there has been in the history of mankind. You just have to have the courage to initiate the process. If you are waiting on successful people to come knocking on your door, forget it; it's not going to happen. They are not going to come to you and say, "Hey, this looks like a great business idea. I'd like to give you some money so you can get going." That's never going to happen. You have got to take the lead and initiate the call.

It's okay if you get rejected. You may get a no. Rejection is part of the process. Not all of my requests for help have come back with positive answers. Remember when I asked Herb Berry if I would ever have an opportunity to own a part of his store? He said, "Absolutely not!"

A lot of people would have stopped at that point, but I knew there had to be a way, so I took my no like a man and went and asked someone else. Herb Berry wasn't the only person alive. I had Roger Street and Dale Garrett, the guys who owned the insurance agency. What if they had told me no? I would have found somebody else. If your dreams are important enough, you will find a way to make them happen. I believe that with every fiber of my being. You have to make your own way.

I got my no from Herb Berry, but his no was just for that moment. I can say that because years later I bought 50 percent of his store. The no I got from him was only temporary. There is no such thing as failure; you either succeed or learn. You've learned something when you don't repeat the things that were not successful.

You have to believe in yourself enough to be able to get past the rejections in life. Life is full of perceived killers of opportunities. There may be circumstances, such as accidents, illnesses, or a myriad of other things, that will get in your way. Temporary setbacks are inevitable, and you should plan to experience them from time to time. Sometimes, you have to step out in faith and just keep moving—even when you don't think you can.

Living by faith in God has played a tremendous part in my journey through life. My faith is by far the most important thing I possess. Trials and tribulations have tested it over the years, but my faith has allowed me to move forward—in spite of whatever obstacle was in my way.

My faith includes total dependency on Christ. As a Christian, I'm a steward of what I have been entrusted to manage. I look to Him every day for divine intervention to guide me, lead me, and direct me in all His ways. God knows what's best, and He will show you exactly what you are to do in every situation, through prayer and Scripture found in the Bible.

My voice shalt thou hear in the morning, O Lord; in the morning will I direct my prayer unto thee, and will look up. Psalm 5:3 (KJV)

I try to spend at least an hour, five days a week, in prayer and meditation. Many days I will end my time listening to praise and worship music, trying to center my thoughts. For years now, I have found it very meaningful to pray for each member of my immediate family, close friends, and immediate clients by name. I want God to inspire, teach, and direct me as how to lead my family and instruct my clients.

I'm not perfect, and I don't pretend to be so. I have many faults and challenges that I face regularly. As we all are striving to be better each day, I am reminded the only way to serve my clients well is to be honest with them and share how I really see their situation. This tactic many times calls for an intense and turbulent conversation. I'm convinced the only way to truly help someone is to be blatantly honest. I used to be pretty cocky and arrogant myself; life has its way of humbling you. Now, I attempt to be somewhat gentler while remaining true to my convictions. I have very challenging conversations with my clients because, oftentimes, I have to tell them very difficult things. When you are searching for a coach or mentor, insist on honest feedback.

As I reflect on the past and anticipate the future, one thing I know for certain: living by faith makes everything in my life work better. I pray, "God, if you don't want us to trek down a certain path, please put up a barrier." Simultaneously, I pray for doors to be opened if I'm headed in the right direction. Doors have been opened my entire adult life that I could have never opened on my own. Time and again, doors get closed; for whatever reason, things don't transpire. When that happens, I say, "Well, you know what? If God doesn't want me to go that way, I'll go the other direction." The important thing is I don't quit moving. I keep going forward and let Him guide me each and every day. It's very exhausting trying to live life under my own power.

That's what it means to live by faith. God doesn't need your help to solve anything. In fact, if you continually get in God's way by trying to solve your own problems, you are actually doing more harm than good. Your faith will be strengthened when it's used; that means you have to allow God to do wonderful things for you so that you trust Him enough to rely on Him more.

A door may open or a door may shut, but in order to keep moving in a forward direction, I let Him guide my path. That is what faith is about for me. Work like it depends on you, and trust like it depends on Him.

LEAN IN . . .

- You need to have quick wins on a regular basis, but the majority of our time should be spent on long-term goals that bring you to a bigger and better place in life.

- Don't do something that would jeopardize the safety of your family, but don't be so conservative that you miss great opportunities.

- If you find it difficult asking other people for assistance, you're not alone. Many have a hard time asking for help because they are afraid of being rejected or they don't want to feel like a burden to someone else. Fear of rejection is at the top of the list as to why people won't ask someone else to help them. When you are honest with those who care about you and are vulnerable and transparent, revealing your weaknesses in a tactful manner, you just arrived at the intersection where strength begins.

- As I reflect on the past and anticipate the future, one thing I know for certain: living by faith makes everything in my life work better.

CHAPTER 3
FINISHED AT TWENTY-SEVEN

It was awkward. I sat at my desk, staring into the eyes of a Fortune 500 company executive. He was leaning forward, sitting on the edge of a new leather sofa in my office. I had a floor-to-ceiling bookshelf just to his left that served as a hidden wall for the company vaults. It was just like something you would see in the movies. To his right was a sixty-inch big screen television. The entire back wall was two-way mirrors that overlooked the showroom. I had a security system so that I could monitor every square foot, including the exterior. At the far end of the office was a full-size bathroom, complete with an oversized shower. I'll have to admit; it was quite the position for a twenty-seven-year-old. We had just completed the construction of a five thousand square foot store, all state of the art. Momentarily, I sat glancing around the room; I could feel the tension mounting. I was feeling anxiety at a level I had never before experienced. "Well," he said, "what do you think"? The question was whether or not I was willing to sell. *What would I do? Where would I go?* He sat back, waiting patiently. He had done this many times, with more than three hundred locations under his belt. He was calm and collected.

People often set goals for when they will shut it all down. They try to visualize when they want to stop working and live a life of convenience and leisure; that's called retirement. You may look to your golden years as the ultimate goal in your journey through life and long for the time of rest.

The thought of retirement was an ever-present state of mind for me. As soon as the necessary funds were available, check out was inevitable. Getting up, leaving, staying, or scheduling my own personal activities was front and center. Little did I know that there would be an opportunity at such a young age.

You guessed it; he waited me out. I quoted a price to get rid of him, but he accepted it. I felt a sense of isolation and depression shortly after selling. I realize right now that's hard to understand, but hopefully, as we go down these trails, you will learn where I am coming from. I now know, I don't ever want to retire again, or at least not entirely! I felt like I had arrived at what I thought was my retirement point when I was twenty-seven years old. My business had just sold, and I had a little money in the bank. Now, utopia, it was time to start living it up!

It's an incredible feeling when you come from nothing, and then, all of a sudden, you wake up on a Monday morning, and you don't have to do anything. I said to myself, "Yes, I'm here. I have arrived. This is awesome! I've got nothing on my schedule. I've got money in the bank. I can stay home; I can play golf; I can go fishing; I can do whatever I want to do." Quite honestly, it felt good for a little while.

What I found, though, through about an eighteen-month process, is when you think you've made it, you often start believing your own press clippings. You start thinking you're invincible. You start thinking everything you touch will turn to gold. You start believing that you are good and have the Midas touch.

I developed a sense of arrogance, pride, and egotism that was unmatched by anyone in his twenties. Looking back, when I would engage in conversations, I would always make sure everyone else knew I had a schedule of flexibility. I could do whatever I wanted, whenever I was ready. When you act that way, people don't hang around long.

Robin and I thought a great start to retirement, coupled with a celebration mindset, would be to take our kids to a friend's place in Naples, Florida. It would be a great way to spend our entire summer as newly retired people. We would have time to decompress; things had been very stressful during the sell. In our dreams, this had been an incredible idea, but in reality, not so much. I was twenty-seven; Robin was twenty-six, and we had two small children, Brooke and Hollie. When we got there, we discovered that everyone our age was at work, just getting out of college, and many just getting out of bed for the day. I mean, seriously, we were young. I rationalized this away, saying to myself, *I've already worked half my life; I started at thirteen.*

There were, however, a bunch of senior adults everywhere. I'd go to the golf course, and the gray hairs would be there playing golf. Talk about feeling out of place; I was asking to play golf with men who were old enough to be my father and, in some cases, old enough to be my grandfather.

The conversations were not gratifying either. They would talk about their ailments and Medicare, and these were not topics that I wanted to discuss. To make matters worse, they were much better golfers than me. They had a lot more experience at golf than I did, and it just wasn't much fun.

Retirement wasn't what I thought it was going to be. It felt different than I had imagined. It felt unexciting. I tried to make it work for a while, but the truth is, you can only play so much golf. Now, if you're a golfer, you may be thinking, *I don't know, that sounds like it would be ideal.* And, it was for a little while. Then it got to a point where my only accomplishment for the day was to shoot a good score. The issue was that nobody cared about what score I shot. Eventually, Robin didn't care, and then I didn't even care. It was like I had nothing to look forward to, even though I was living the life I thought I had wanted.

When you work every day, you get excited about your time off. You plan vacations that you look forward to for months. There are those times when you think, *I'm going to leave the office and get things off my mind. I get to rest and rejuvenate and then come back to work reenergized and ready to go.* All of that went away for me, because every day, every hour, I could just choose to do what I wanted. All the excitement and anticipation of a much-needed vacation appeared to be gone. I was not interested in taking time off because I was on a permanent holiday.

It sounds a little bit funny describing it this way because most people are at work, and they're stressed and anxious, and they want to get away from there. I'm just speaking from the experience of having been out of that routine and having had the opportunity to plan each day as I chose. It just doesn't give you what you think it will.

> I thought I had found life, but in reality, I had lost my purpose in life.

Over time, I quit playing golf as much. Going fishing became more of a chore than a pastime. Finding a buddy to go with took longer than the activity. Then isolation started setting in. It wasn't fun because I wasn't sharing that experience with anyone. Robin came with me once in a while, and it was fun with her, but then even that stopped. I was looking for guy talk when I was fishing, and it just wasn't available. Slowly, the things I enjoyed and looked forward to didn't have the same meaning.

I spent a lot of time pondering my decision. The truth is, I had lost my purpose. Purpose is the driving, motivating force that propels us to significance. Without it, we get lost in our efforts to find or create happiness and contentment. I thought I had found life, but in reality, I had lost my purpose in life. I had the opportunity to access an unlimited supply of fun, yet I felt more unfulfilled than I ever had been in my life. I had experienced great hardship, and now I was without a schedule or responsibilities, and I was more miserable than ever. I could not get my arms around this. What I was feeling made no common sense whatsoever. I thought I had completely lost my mind. Why could I not be excited about where I was in life?

That led to a sense of depression. I'm not talking clinical depression; there wasn't medication or a psychiatrist or anything like that, but I was depressed and in a state that I'd never experienced. I didn't understand it. How had I gotten to the point that I had lost my joy?

At this stage in my life, I didn't have advisors or people I trusted helping me to discover what the problem was or how to find a solution. I truthfully had never even considered getting advice from someone. Asking for assistance was a foreign concept to me. I thought you were just supposed to burrow in and do the best you knew how.

When I was depressed, I ate more, and that made me want to sleep more. The more I slept, the more boredom set in. The more bored I was, the more I wanted to eat, which made me gain weight, and then more sleep was required. A vicious cycle developed that could drain the life out of a person faster than anything else I had ever experienced. It felt like I was in a rut with no escape. No one was there pushing or challenging me.

I got to the point where I'd get up, lie around the house, sit on the porch, maybe play golf, come back, and take a nap. It got so bad that my wife Robin had to step in and set me straight. She woke me up one day from a nap and said, "Something's gotta change because this is not you." She told me I had to go back to work or start another company—just do something. I wasn't fun to be around anymore because I was depressed and unhappy, not to mention I was fifty pounds overweight.

What turned things around for me was the realization that I had a purpose on this planet, and that purpose was bigger than fulfilling the selfish desires of my own heart. You will not be happy if your whole purpose in life is to waste the day away doing nothing, day in and day out. There is no gratification in doing things only for yourself.

Go to the ant, you sluggard; consider its ways and be wise! It has no commander, no overseer or ruler, yet it stores its provisions in summer and gathers its food at harvest. How long will you lie there, you sluggard? When will you get up from your sleep?—Proverbs 6:6–9

Think about what happens when people lose their spouse to death. The survivors go home every day to an empty house. No one knows if they made it back or not. No one is waiting for them. No one depends on them. They don't cook for anybody but themselves, so there is no excitement in preparing meals. There is no joy in doing the yard or keeping a garden because they are doing it for themselves. When you become the only one benefitting from your existence, life can become dull and mundane. Don't hear me wrong; there are millions of single senior adults living a vibrant life, adding tons of value to society. However, there are also those who become so self-centered that everything they do revolves around them. This is when we become self-absorbed and purposeless.

There is so much meaning, gratification, and excitement in life when we are doing things for others. I didn't have that perspective when I was twenty-seven years old. It was all about me. It was all about Aaron and his selfish desires. I was on a quest for ease. We are not made to be in isolation with a central focus on ourselves. We are designed to be in community with an ever-present mindfulness of others. It is so much more rewarding when you have a desire to provide for, care for, encourage, and empower a friend or loved one. When you live your life looking to help someone else, you've got a purpose. There's meaning in your life. There's a reason you exist.

This is why it's important to have people you trust who can help guide you through tough spots in your life. I look back and see I didn't know that I needed trusted, unbiased advisors in my life. It was a foreign concept to me. Like most people, I thought I should keep everything private. God forbid you let anyone know that you don't have all the answers.

Many times, we're taught to protect our interests, and sometimes that means not letting other people close enough to help us. You don't share your business or your faults. You hide behind an imaginary veil so that your peers won't know the truth. You build a facade so that you will appear to be someone you're not. As men, we think we need to have this alpha-male persona that shows massive strength, and in reality, it's just the opposite. People who let their veil down and invite trusted advisors into their lives soon subject themselves to the scrutiny of a trusted few, and then they realize that's where the power lies, in honesty.

I thought I could not show any of my cards. I couldn't tell people if I didn't understand something. I was afraid they would think I was uneducated or unwise, that I didn't know what I was doing. You may have some of those same fears, but I can tell you it's the exact opposite.

Now, I'm older and hope to be a little

People want to be around individuals who are real. wiser. I see clearly the more I engage in significant relationships while maintaining honesty and transparency, the better I become. People want to be with those who are genuine. I would suggest that the faster you let down that imaginary veil and let people know you intimately, the more quickly you are able to build lasting relationships that will serve you well long-term. People want to be around individuals who are real.

I didn't trust myself to other people when I was younger; it felt strange, and I didn't give it much thought. No one was there to tell me, "Hey, you need to have a plan because, at twenty-seven, you're going to feel invincible. You're going to become arrogant; you're going to become prideful; and that's not going to serve you well." I found myself isolated, and I let pride get in the way of my significance. You see, I didn't even know these things because I was not around others who cared. I was not investing in others like I know how to do now. I suppose some of this is healthy maturity. We need to eradicate those things that trip us up, and that can only be done if we surround ourselves with the counsel of wise people.

For lack of guidance a nation falls, but victory is won through many advisers.— Proverbs 11:14

I realized I had to make a change; things were not going well at home. Earlier I mentioned that Robin suggested I get a job or create another start-up. Knowing me now for over a decade, she knew I had to do something productive to be my best self. The next day, I scheduled an appointment to visit with Herb Berry, my employer as a teenager. We had stayed in contact pretty regularly over the past nine years, for different reasons, but primarily because we were in the same business and we were only a few miles apart. Eighteen months after I retired, I was back to where I started, asking Herb for a job. He laughed at first and said, "Big A, are you already out of money?" (Herb is the one who nicknamed me Big A in 1974, and it stuck.)

I said, "No, I'm not out of money, but I'm bored, depressed, and I have got to do something with my time. I know you're working here every day, with no ability to take a day off. Why don't you let me help? You can pay me to work one or two days a week and then you can take some time for yourself."

He liked that idea. He was going through a tough time in his own life, and he felt this would be mutually beneficial for the two of us. It was a perfect time for him to be able to step away from the store to get a much-needed break.

Shortly after I started working with Herb, I made him an offer to help grow his company. I said, "Hey, I've got some money from the sale of my business that I want to invest, so why don't I loan it to you, and we'll grow this business to the next level?" I started lending the company money, and we started increasing our profits very quickly. It started growing as a result of the cash infusion, and as time went on, I started getting in pretty deep with the money I was loaning the company.

I approached Herb again, and this time, I told him we should partner up. He thought about it and eventually agreed, and I bought half the company. This is the company that he had told me ten years prior I would never own. I get tickled thinking about that sometimes. Ten years after Herb said I would never own any part of his business, I owned 50 percent. You never know what God's going to do and how things will work out.

I was back. I now had a reason to get up in the morning and get going. The creativity and energy were flowing, and this time, I was better than ever. You see, I had a new outlook on life. I now understood that I needed a purpose, and I needed to allow myself to be interested in more than just my superficial wants.

My identity changed. I let go of who I thought I should be and realized I needed to turn to and rely on God first and foremost. I needed to focus on who God had called me to be. If you take nothing else from this book, please take this: your identity should be tied up in Christ, period.

What happens if your title or your possessions are suddenly taken away? If that was to happen, you might start to believe you are no one and you have no value, which is a lie. We wrongly base our identity on what we can do, rather than upon what God has done in His sovereign grace for each one of us.

No, in all these things we are more than conquerors through Him who loved us.— Romans 8:37 (BSB)

But you are a chosen people, a royal priesthood, a holy nation, God's special possession, that you may declare the praises of Him who called you out of darkness into His wonderful light.—1 Peter 2:9 (BSB)

Think about it: if you're worth a million dollars and your identity is tied up in your possessions and you do a good business deal so that you become worth two million dollars, does that mean, as a person, you're now worth twice as much? Or let's go the other way. You're worth a million dollars, and you lose it all; does that mean you're worthless? Of course not, but that is one of the great lies we believe. This way of thinking can ultimately derail you on your way to success. It's the same way with a job title. It's been amazing to me over the years to see how tied to a title people are. Titles can be equally important to people with money. They want to be able to say, "I'm the general manager," or "I'm the COO," or "I'm the CFO." Think about it. When men meet someone for the first time, they will usually ask two questions: "What's your name?" and "What do you do?"

My good friend Bob Warren had an excellent way to answer these questions. When people would ask him what his name was and what he did, he would respond with, "My name is Bob. I'm a Christ follower, and I assist others in transforming their lives." His identity is tied up in Christ and not in his occupation. We put so much value on the stuff, and we shouldn't. When those things go away, it will put us in a deep depression because we have all of our identity tied up in something that is never stable.

Here's the part of this book where I may lose you, and if you feel that this is not something you're interested in, I ask you to keep an open mind and listen to this next part anyway. We have to put our total reliance and dependence on Jesus Christ, and from that point, recognize the fact that we're not owners but stewards over what He has entrusted us with. You have to get yourself into the mindset that you are a steward and not an owner.

The truth is, you're not in charge. When you are a person of faith, you are aware that God is in charge. I thought I was, but my wayward thinking led to bad decisions and self-centeredness. I had no one to answer to, and honestly, I felt accomplished in what I had done and achieved.

When we recognize that everything is a gift from God and we are undeserving from our own merits, we simply view everything from a different perspective. Our values change, and we take better care of things that are most important: our time, money, gifts, and talents. I'm convinced that God entrusts a little to us to see how we steward and manage what He has given. If we prove to manage that well, then He increases the conduit size. If He can't trust you with a little, how can He trust you with a lot?

The man who had received five bags of gold brought the other five. "Master," he said, "you entrusted me with five bags of gold. See, I have gained five more."—Matthew 25:20

Some people have what appears to be great success, but that doesn't necessarily mean it's from God. You can be successful in the world's view without God's help, but how much more can you have *with* God's help? I want to be a steward over what He's entrusted me with. I want to manage well the relationships, resources, and finances that He's brought to me. I want to manage those things adequately and appropriately. I can't do that with an ownership mentality.

If your identity is tied up in your career and the job goes away, where does that leave you? There is a way to relinquish that and lean on God. The Bible tells us to lean not on our understanding but trust in Him. That means you need to get to a point that you can honestly say, "Whatever the outcome, I'm going to trust You [God]." That's a very hard place to get to. It's tough to have that blind trust, but the great thing about faith is that the more it's exercised, the stronger it gets. As Christ followers, He gives us a guidebook or a map. I mentioned it earlier; it's called *the Bible.*

Carnally speaking, we can't understand its Truth because we don't have the mind of God. God can see around the corner; He knows what's coming; He protects us from things; He shields us at times, more than we can know. If we could see as God sees, in black and white, we wouldn't need faith. There is a dependency we must have on our Creator. When you are in that mindset, you quit fearing what other people say because you are following the divine intervention of God in your life.

That's why you should read Scripture [the Bible] daily, and that's why you have to put your dependency on and in Jesus Christ. He will give us a renewed strength each and every day. There's no way I could do that on my own. I don't have the experience; I don't have the wisdom; I don't have the knowledge; I don't have the ability that Christ gives me every single day. But when I rely on Him to help and guide me, I find that I have everything I need to keep moving forward.

So in my twenty-seventh year, when everything seemed like it was going well, it just wasn't going right. I changed my focus and let my identity in Christ shape my choices. That decision means that even when everything might not be going well, it's always going right because I have my focus in the correct place.

For God so loved the world that He gave His only begotten Son, that whoever believes in Him should not perish but have everlasting life.—John 3:16 (KJV)

LEAN IN . . .

- When you think you've made it, you often start believing your own press clippings.

- Purpose is the driving, motivating force that propels us to significance. Without it, we get lost in our efforts to find or create happiness and contentment.

- People want to be with those who are genuine. I would suggest that the faster you let down that imaginary veil and let people know you intimately, the more quickly you are able to build lasting relationships that will serve you well long-term.

- The great thing about faith is that the more it's exercised, the stronger it gets.

C H A P T E R 4
BREAKING FREE

L ife is constantly changing. Think about this: you are never the same today as you were yesterday. In one way or the other, you will be different each and every day. As time goes on, you will continue to change, sometimes for the better, sometimes not. The natural progression of life takes its toll, but many changes are the result of our choices. While not all change is good, transitions in life are not necessarily a bad thing either. Sometimes those periods of transition lead us into phenomenal transformations.

Going into partnership with Herb Berry was one of those transitional times that led to transformation for me. I was coming off that brief retirement phase where I basically shut everything down. I had been exhausted. I was ready to get back into the grind, but I was not quite ready to go back to working ten-to-twelve-hour days. Herb and I discussed it and came up with a solution that would be beneficial for the both of us. We both had families we wanted to spend more time with, so we decided to each work three days a week.

It was unbelievable. I couldn't even imagine having the kind of schedule where I could work three days and be off four. For me, it was the ideal situation for transitioning from an eighteen-month sabbatical. We started working this schedule, and before I realized what had happened, nine years passed.

It would have been very easy at this time to have allowed myself to increase my workload because business was very good, and who doesn't want "more"? It's so easy to rationalize to yourself, and to those who love you, that the extra hours will only be for a brief time. The next thing you know, you are sucked into the abyss, the black hole. I feel as though I made the right decision. I could have made considerably more money, but on this go around, I was seeking lifestyle and freedom, not just more cash. By this time, Herb and I were veterans in the pawn business, and that made it easy for each of us to take care of our responsibilities and move forward. There really wasn't much that either of us needed from the other; we knew the business, and nothing suffered with the absence of the other. It was pretty sweet!

Prior to this new arrangement, I was an "all in" type of guy. When I started my business at eighteen, I let the desires of my flesh drive me to work all the time. I was singularly focused on building the best business possible, which is not really a bad objective. When I decided to take the "early retirement option," I shut everything down in a ninety-day period and then did nothing. I guess you could say I am an extremist; this has its benefits, but it can also have disadvantages. I let the current circumstances dictate how my life went. This time it was different; I wanted balance in my life. I wanted to work and be useful at the same time. I wanted to have meaning and purpose while simultaneously spending quality time with my family, something I had neglected previously.

> You need balance, or some semblance of balance, in your life.

You need balance, or some semblance of balance, in your life. However, this is most difficult to master. The quest for balance is elusive at times, and it creates havoc for personal and professional relationships. Everyone is always vying for your time. I have one very important suggestion for you. Embrace the tension; it's never going away completely. No matter how vast your pool of resources, this feeling will never go away. As long as you feel the tension, you probably are attempting to do the right thing. The tension is similar to a governor on an automobile. It limits how fast you might go; it's a built-in indicator. Professionals are striving each day to be successful at work, and you should too, but every day, these same professionals are sacrificing their families on the altar of accomplishment, prestige, and money.

Pay attention here: don't invest all your quality time in making a living. Business owners and corporate executives often choose unwisely in this situation, and my heart's desire is for you not to be added to those miserable casualties of losing your family for the sake of advancement. We use the excuse that our family deserves better than we had and we're going to give them the life that we never had. Without question, you signed up to provide for your family, but money is not the only thing that needs to be provided. You need to offer love, security, strength, leadership, and moral guidance. Teaching integrity and character attributes will go a lot further than a few extra bucks. When you choose a semi-balanced lifestyle over selfish aspirations, something interesting happens. You become very proactive and very focused on things that really are important. When you become laser focused, an inch wide and a mile deep in impactful areas of your life, you tend to master the objective.

My newfound schedule was a great switch for me because it allowed me to have an ample amount of free time. I was able to go to the girls' ball games, Girl Scout activities, and cheerleading competitions. I need to confess one thing. I dreaded the time of year when Girl Scout cookies went on sale. I despised setting up tables in the heat of the day at the entrance of K-mart, but I did it. When my professional responsibilities only required three days a week, it offered up many more opportunities for family events. I realize that you may not have such a flexible schedule right now, and I get that, but if you want that kind of lifestyle, you have to make choices early on that allow you to at least head in that direction.

There are so many times we want that instant gratification; we want to get to the finish line before the race has even begun. If you can have a long-term outlook on what you want and be very specific in determining the things that are important to you today, you will be able to choose your schedule long-term. It's hard. I don't want to imply that this lifestyle comes easily because it doesn't. There are seasons in our lives that we second-guess whether or not the sacrifice is worth it. I want you to lend me your ear for a moment. I have something I want to whisper to you. Turn your head; close your eyes. I have three little words for you: It's worth it!

We all have these grandiose dreams and goals. You long for the day you have your mortgage paid off. Well, to do that, maybe the new car purchase has to wait. It's just the little decisions we make now that allow us to have exactly what we want in the future. Most people don't decide what they want early enough. They don't even know what they want. They just know they want more. They want bigger, faster, and shinier. Have you ever considered that *more* may not be best for you? How is making your business bigger making your life better?

Sometimes there are great benefits to expansion, and other times, it's a distraction. Maybe you're just caught up living the life that your mom or dad wanted you to live, or you're trying to keep up with the lives of your neighbors. If at all possible, be genuine to yourself and chase your own legacy. It's so refreshing to see unique perspectives and creative ways of living out your full potential. Attempt to eradicate any thoughts of living your life the way other people think you should and have the courage and stamina to stay focused on what you want. It is possible to have the lifestyle you design. If that's working three to four days a week, you just might have to eliminate some of the nonessentials; we can't have everything. Avoiding debt as much as possible and living below your means is a great start to getting what you want in the end.

Mindset is paramount to success. Carol Dweck wrote a great book called *MindSet*, in which she explains the value of growth over a fixed mindset. You may not be able to do something today, but with the proper education, training, and the correct way of thinking, you just may be able to do it tomorrow. Without this frame of reference, we certainly limit our possibilities. As it turns out, I was in dire need of a growth mindset. Herb and I came to the stark realization that our present location was inadequate to support the two of us; we simply were undersized. Berry's had been in their present location for twenty years, and we were turning everything upside down. Were we nervous? Absolutely.

There was a Dollar Thrift Store that had been open for decades; we needed this space. When I first thought about what the possibility of getting it might be, the first thing that ran through my mind was, zero. There was not a snowball's chance of getting this store. So, off I went on a relentless quest to purchase this location. Much to my surprise, the owner turned out to be none other than the H. G. Hill Company, the largest property owner at that time in Davidson County. Mr. Hill owned a chain of grocery stores in the Nashville area, but he made his fortune in the real estate business. What really made this difficult was Mr. Hill had a reputation for never selling his properties. I made an offer anyway. Hey, you never know. Just as I suspected, a resounding

> You have to have the personal grit, determination, and perseverance to trudge through heartache and trials to succeed at a high level.

no came back within twenty-four hours. No counteroffer, no negotiations, no interest at all, just a thunderous no. I would say that the majority of the businessmen I know would have ended their efforts at that juncture. Most people aren't willing to fight for what they want, and in my case, for what I desperately needed. Without this building, I was in big trouble. Don't be the person who says, "I'll do anything to succeed," and then bails out at the first sign of difficulty. Listen, if you want something badly enough, you have to have the persistence it takes to get it. You have to have the personal grit, determination, and perseverance to trudge through heartache and trials to succeed at a high level. Those are all key ingredients for success.

For me, no has always just meant no for that day; it doesn't mean no forever. Most people take no as the final answer. Don't you be that person! When the real estate representatives of the H. G. Hill Company finally met with me, I knew there was an outside possibility we had a chance. We met at the actual location, and the first thing one of the representatives said after our introductions was, "We don't normally sell our properties." I was trying to be polite and tactical at the same time. I'll be the first one to admit; I was way outgunned. These guys had bought more property than I will ever even attempt to. My very first thought was, what else can we do if buying it is not an option?

Prayer, coupled with an insistent attitude, revealed halfway through our conversation another possibility: a 1031 exchange. I was vaguely familiar with this as I had traded properties on another deal, years before. Once they agreed to this, I waited until they found a comparable property, bought it, and then exchanged it for the one I needed. This exercise was tiring and complicated, but it worked. Many times in business, we run into the least bit of resistance and throw in the towel. Spend the energy and effort to exhaust all possibilities.

Always remember that there are other ways of accomplishing your task, rather than relying on conventional ways of thinking. If I had quit at "no," we would have never gotten it. That's why I call that story "Ten Thousand Square Feet of Miracles."

As a person of faith, I prefer to follow, as best I know how, the leadership of God. Many times this path is difficult to discern, and I'm certain I have not always perfectly followed His ideal plan. I'm a carnal being, and I fail many times, but when you allow God to be in control, He will direct your path. He will close doors that need to be closed and open ones that lead to where He wants you to be. All you have to do is stop fighting Him and start following Him. In my situation with the building, I was able to say, "Okay, He's got another plan, so we'll shift our focus and go down that road." The end result does not always work out the way we want; that's why we trust in a Higher Power. If you could always see the end result, faith would be unnecessary.

Trust in the LORD with all your heart and lean not on your own understanding.— Proverbs 3:5

It worked. We got the building we needed, and our business began to grow. I had a dream schedule, and financially, I was positioned well.

I was able to hire more staff and delegate the things I needed to. I had traded a job for a business. This meant I could go on vacation and still continue to make money. I didn't have to be there each and every day. I wasn't a slave to my job any more, and I wasn't trading time for money. I once again was in full motion.

I had the opportunity to create the lifestyle I had chosen, rather than continuing to focus on just making more money. I could have continued to be there every day, growing the business bigger and pouring the money I made back in it to add more stores, but that's not what I wanted. I wanted a better lifestyle, one that would give me more time to be around my kids and one that would allow me to be engaged with them as they grew up.

Making more money is the traditional focus. I want to encourage you to broaden your horizon, to open your mind and reflect on the possibilities of your current situation. I don't want you to think that money is the solution to all of your problems. The relentless pursuit of more money can lead to the destruction of the most important things in your life.

It's good to have money and the desire to make more money isn't inherently evil, but you have to ask yourself these questions: What do I want to make more money for? What do I want to do with the money when I make it? How is making my business bigger going to make my life better? How is creating wealth going to impact my family and others around me? Is working longer hours to make more money going to put me in more bondage or free me up to enjoy life?

The relentless pursuit of more money can lead to the destruction of the most important things in your life.

Everything you do, all the decisions you make, require your time and energy. So where do you want your time spent? You have to be very intentional and make those decisions early on. I could have had more money today, but I would have forfeited countless memories. There are trade-offs in everything, and for me, lifestyle for that season was more important than money.

Being intentional impacts every aspect of your life, even in building relationships. I don't believe in chance meetings, and I have one for the record books. There was a Madison Chamber of Commerce breakfast meeting that I attended in the summer of 1995. At this particular meeting, they invited a guest speaker, Dave Ramsey, the host of *The Money Game,* which was relatively new to the Nashville scene. The show's message was how to get out of debt and invoke something rare when it comes to money: common sense. He seemed like a pretty cool guy, so I went up and introduced myself. I told him about the new store we had just opened and explained it tied into what he was teaching people about getting rid of things they didn't want and being frugal with their money. I invited him to stop by on his way back to Franklin, and he did. We had just opened the store, and it was absolutely beautiful. Dave said this was just the type of place he was looking for to advertise on his new show. Dave was and continues to be a strong advocate for being debt-free. Under no circumstance would he promote pawning anything, but he would strongly suggest buying there at discounted prices.

I told him I didn't want to advertise with him because his show was fairly new, only three years old. If you knew Dave, you could understand this better; he was very persistent and would not even consider taking no as a real answer. He has the ability to sell, which I admired. He offered to give me a week for free just to try it out. I figured I had nothing to lose, so I took him up on it. At that time, you could do a live ad and talk about your merchandise on air with Dave every day. I had never done anything like this and was nervous, but I decided to try the live ads. Dave and I would talk on air about what was on special at an appointed time each day. This went on for a few days, and all of a sudden, we had a whole new group of people coming into the store. I realized quickly that Dave had built a tribe of loyal listeners. In just a few days, I had made enough money that the decision was easy to sign an annual contract with Dave. To this day, Berry's still advertises with him.

Let's fast forward a few years. I was at a Mercy Me Christian concert at the Curb Center in Nashville. Dave Ramsey happened to be attending the same event and was sitting just ahead of me. He walked up during intermission and told me he wanted me to pray about joining his personal mastermind that he, Ron Doyle, and Dan Miller were starting. We would be meeting in person in Dave's conference room just off his private office. The three of them had been in a Christian Leadership Concepts (CLC) group for two years, and they wanted to continue meeting and thought a mastermind was the best option. I had no idea what he was talking about and told him I had never heard of anything like this before. He explained I just needed to trust him on this and experience a place where high achievers meet every week to do life together.

I started thinking about the pros and cons. By this time, I had been friends with Dave for almost a decade. Dave's tenacity in all he does was very alluring. He's a man of high character, with morals that are uncompromised. At the time, I didn't know the other men, but I respected Dave enough to know he would select honorable men, so I went. The mastermind was comprised of ten very diverse, yet very similar, men. It was a little bit awkward at first, but very quickly it started feeling like a safe place for me. Because we were in Franklin, thirty minutes away from home, these were not my inner circle of friends, and that dynamic had its benefits. Right from the start, it allowed me to be more honest and transparent without the fear of others—mainly my close friends—knowing my personal state of affairs. I started really enjoying my time with them. It almost felt like I had my own board of directors. They became trusted advisors, who I knew would tell me the truth. After all, they had nothing to gain or lose by whatever they told me, so why would they not tell me the truth?

When I got involved with this mastermind, I wasn't a reader and had limited interest in personal development. Now, I'm an avid and passionate reader. More than 10 percent of my gross revenue annually goes towards education and personal training. I hire specific trainers, coaches, and educators to further my knowledge. I attend multiple conferences each year and push myself past my upper-limit challenges.

My mastermind group has read hundreds of books together over the years, and it has been time well spent. Roundtable discussions were lively. Varying educational backgrounds from high school diplomas to PhDs were represented, with me being the high school graduate. We had a couple of local pastors, which added a very unique twist to theology; we had lively debates often centered around our faith. Ken Abraham, a nationally recognized author with multiple appearances on the *New York Times* Bestseller list and now over 110 books to his credit, was a part of our group.

When we started the mastermind, Ken didn't have this many titles, nor was Dave Ramsey on nearly six hundred radio stations. That's the magic of the mastermind. We all had a dream to advance our careers, and we were able to lock arms and encourage one another forward. Dan Miller was just starting his world-renowned program based on his book

48 Days to the Work You Love. I got to watch these businesses unfold, and it taught me how to do my business well. Surrounding yourself with world-class individuals, not necessarily famous people, just world-class, will empower you like nothing else.

Business was front and center, but we spent an inordinate amount of time discussing personal challenges as well. Family is very important to each of these men, and we felt it incumbent upon us to excel in that arena of our lives also. We worked through many challenges within our respected families, and we celebrated huge victories together.

I fell in love with that process. I was able to subject myself to the scrutiny of those men who grew to love each other deeply. The veil came down early on with me because I couldn't be a fake any longer. I had been fake in many areas of my life previously. Why would I want to do that? Why would I want to drive thirty minutes and spend an hour and a half in a room with a bunch of men and be a fake? It taught me it was okay to be vulnerable, and it taught me to be transparent. The transparency actually made me stronger because it allowed me to work on my weaknesses.

That period brought on a number of changes in my life. Jim Rohn says we are the average of the five people that we surround ourselves with. I thought, *How much better could I be if I double that and associate myself with ten great men?*

And it all started with going to a Chamber of Commerce breakfast. Actually, I don't even like Chamber of Commerce meetings. It seems so artificial to stand around and act interested in someone else just to get his business. My motivation was to build relationships for varying reasons, not to get more customers for the pawnshop.

My primary objective for sharing this story is to encourage you to get into the mix. You can learn at home or the office. There is so much information available online, but what you can't do from home is interact personally. You can't shake hands, grab a shoulder, or give a smile. Good things don't come knocking on your door; you have to go to it. That's the reason I strive to be proactive in just about everything I've done. Who would come to you and say, "Hey, you need to get out of that house and come be with us?" If you're going to be successful financially and in your relationships, you need to be around people who are successful financially and in their relationships.

I was a member of Old Hickory Country Club for about ten years, but it wasn't to be prestigious. It wasn't necessarily to work on my golf game, although I did improve. (I got my handicap to a nine, pretty good for a hacker.) I joined that club to put myself around people who owned local companies, the decision makers and influencers, because they were there on a regular basis. You just have to get into the game, and you can't do that sitting at home on the couch. You've got to go to meetings, conferences, and retreats. I go to three to four conferences a year, and every time I go, I build new relationships. I would even be so bold as to say that the average ROI (return on investment) is ten times the overall cost. When I build new relationships, it helps me be more successful, not only in personal development but financially as well because you get into the mix of the people who are out there doing transactions. An important lesson to learn is always build relationships proactively.

When I met Dave in 1995, we were already doing pretty well. The pawnshop was successful, but we lacked marketing skills. We had a good product, and service that was second to none, just not everyone knew about us. When we signed on to Dave's show, it was the perfect vehicle to share our message and services. Our exact avatar was listening to Dave's show daily. They were frugal, intentional, and proactive in searching for the best value. So, we went from success to major success. We found our perfect niche. In the past, we were taking the shotgun approach to marketing; we were talking to everyone. Well, everyone wasn't interested, but Dave's audience was. The truth is, if you are talking to everyone, you are talking to no one. Identify your audience.

Greg McKeown talks about being an inch wide and a mile deep, and that's what we were able to do. We were able to take our market-ing dollars and put them into a vehicle that reached out and touched the per-son that we wanted to speak to. Instead of being an inch deep and a mile wide, we stopped talking to the whole world, and we started talking only to our audience. We became even more successful as a result of talking to those who needed to hear our voice.

Success always breeds opportunity

Success always breeds opportunity. People take notice; they want to be around you. Obviously something you're doing is working, and they want to be a part of that. It's a great responsibility to be in that position, so be mindful that when you do have success, it does breed more opportunity, all the while creating greater responsibility for you to manage well.

I believe joining a mastermind and/or an accountability group is time well invested. There are so many safeguards associated with sur-rounding yourself with the right, trusted advisors. As your business prospers or your status in the community increases, you are more sus-ceptible to falling into the trap of prideful thinking. Sometimes when success comes your way, you start believing that you're invincible, and that can cause you to run off the track. Having those trusted advisors will help you stay centered and focused on the goals that you've set for your life.

This is one of those "I wish I knew then what I know now" types of moments. Early on, I didn't have a mastermind group or accountability group to rely on, and looking back, I can't even begin to imagine how different my life would look now if I did. Isolation is an enemy of excellence. I'll talk more about mastermind groups later in the book, but the main thing I want you to understand for now is to be very mindful of the people you bring into your inner circle. You have to be wise in choosing the people you place trust in. That goes for mastermind groups, advisors, coaches, and even partners.

LEAN IN . . .

- The quest for balance is elusive at times, and it creates havoc for personal and professional relationships. Everyone is always vying for your time. I have one very important suggestion for you. Embrace the tension; it's never going away completely.

- If at all possible, be genuine to yourself and chase your own legacy. It's so refreshing to see unique perspectives and creative ways of living out your full potential. Attempt to eradicate any thoughts of living your life the way other people think you should and have the courage and stamina to stay focused on what you want.

- Don't be the person who says, "I'll do anything to succeed," and then bails out at the first sign of difficulty. Listen, if you want something badly enough, you have to have the persistence it takes to get it.

- If you're going to be successful financially and in your relationships, you need to be around people who are successful financially and in their relationships.

- Isolation is an enemy of excellence.

CHAPTER 5
SETTING BOUNDARIES

I found myself in a newly formed partnership with Herb Berry. Now, I was fortunate enough back then to know Herb, and I knew that we could work together, but as with any partnership, we had to establish certain boundaries and rules. It is important to set rules and guidelines when you're partnering with someone because a soured association can be harder to dissolve than a bad marriage. I know; I have had a couple of partnerships that could stand a redo. When a financial relationship goes south, it will take you to places you don't want to go and keep you longer than you want to stay. You need to make sure you align yourself with people who have high values and strong moral convictions and who have the same goals in life as you do. Make sure your long-term objectives are the same.

You always want to have an operating agreement that spells out each person's role. I even recommend having a buyout agreement that keeps you in line with that person and makes it easy to figure out how to end the partnership when the time comes, and it usually does. The main thing is to always keep communication open.

I will be the first to tell you there are many benefits to partnering with the right person. You can share the workload. You can bounce ideas off one another. You're able to share the financial burden, and you don't have to go it alone. You will have someone to lean on when things get tough. If set up correctly, a partnership can last a lifetime, but if you don't approach it with the utmost care and preparation, it can be one of the most maddening things you'll ever experience.

Fifty percent of all my stress in business has always been the partner and not the client. This is one of the very reasons why I say you have to make sure you align yourself with people who complement you well. It is too difficult to clone yourself, and you don't need to. Just like in a marriage, you want to make sure you are entering the arrangement based on more than just looks and feelings. You have to be sure the person you are partnering with is heading in the same direction for the same reasons you are.

The problems come when you don't find the right person or you partner for the wrong reasons. Move in the direction of partnership with great caution. There is a litany of considerations: Do you share common lifestyles? Is morality a high priority? Are your ethical standards and character values aligned? Do you share common ground with work schedules and time with the family? All these ideas seem unimportant initially—until it's time to make a critical professional decision. Then, all of a sudden, they all come into play.

You may get up at five o'clock and arrive at the office at six, while your partner may not get in until nine o'clock or so. That may be okay for a while, but later you're going to feel like you're pulling more of the load. He may take three vacations, and you only take two, so that leaves you feeling like he is a slacker. Maybe he wants his children to come into the business, and the children may not have values that align with you, but the partner is going almost always to side with his children and not the business, so now you've got a serious conflict. Maybe you want to pour all the money back into the business, and he wants to take the money out and live the American dream. What if your partner dies and then you have his spouse or significant other as your associate? What are you going to do now?

Take time when deciding on your business model; there are so many dynamics to a partnership. People think, *Oh, it would be great to go into business with my buddy from high school. We played football together, and this is going to be so much fun, and everything will be amazing.* They don't give any consideration to all the things I've just talked about, and that is a disaster in the making.

I went into a partnership with three of my best friends: Karl, Drew, and Eddie. We had previously owned a small stock investment company called 4 Investments, LLC. We bought a condo in Destin, Florida, at the Silver Beach Towers during preconstruction for $585,000. It was in 2006, just before the massive crash. It was pretty pricey at the time, but it should have been. It was on the twelfth floor facing the beach, and was an outstanding unit in every regard; it was beautiful. I said, "Before we do this, I want to remain friends long-term, so we're going to have an operating agreement as to what each one of us is going to do. It will spell out what role we each will play."

The agreement turned out to be a seven-page document, and at first, they thought it was a little bit ridiculous. I said, "If we know the rules of the game to start with, there's going to be no hard feelings, but if we go into it with all these unanswered questions, there's a lot of room for conflict."

The questions that were used in building the agreement were all good questions and covered all the possible scenarios that we could think of that would come up once we entered into this partnership.

They included things like the following: If I want to get out, when can I get out? How are you going to pay me? Who has first right of refusal? If one of my guests tears up the place, are we going to split that cost, or am I going to pay for it? When are we going to sell it? If our grown children want to come and stay, when can they come? How much do they pay? How do we split up the holidays?

The operating agreement proved to be successful many times. We are all still close friends. Many businesspeople have fallen to the standard reply: he's my friend; an agreement is not necessary for our relationship. I want to remind you that your enemies are not doing business with you, only your friends. It is essential.

These are the same kinds of questions you should ask before going into any partnership. The questions need to be answered prepartnership, rather than in the middle of an ongoing organization, because it will solve a lot of conflicts, or even better, it will keep the conflicts from ever arising in the first place. If you have these types of questions answered and an agreement in place, it can work well, but if you don't have them in place, it will likely be a disaster.

You have to be able to put boundaries in place. I'm a huge proponent of looking outside the box. I think we all have to do it to reach heights that seem to be out of our grasp, but creating healthy boundaries is a key to long-term success. If you establish your boundaries from the beginning, you set the tone for your business model. It's very similar to having a mission, vision, and value statement.

...creating healthy boundaries is a key to long-term success.

You are intentionally adhering to standards that you established so that everyone can weigh each decision and choose the betterment of the organization. It's the same way with boundaries and why they need to be set up from the start. I would encourage you to set personal and professional boundaries and try to enlist other people to hold you accountable to following each one.

I'll share a couple of my boundaries. Social media platforms are crucial to a lifestyle business. As a life and business coach, I'm always posting content on Facebook, Twitter, and LinkedIn. I have thousands of followers that I interact with regularly. However, I don't do any social media interactions with women. There are none on my Twitter, Facebook, or LinkedIn. I do have some women followers, but I do not have control over who follows me. The main reason I don't have interaction with the ladies is I only mentor/coach male clients; women are not my ideal customer, so there's no need for communication. I'm not saying it's bad to communicate with ladies by any means, and I have absolutely nothing against women. I'm just saying, for me, it's a boundary, very intentionally set. I don't go to lunch one-on-one with a lady. I typically carbon copy my assistant on all email correspondence with women. I'm never alone with women, ever. I don't take photographs one-on-one with ladies. They don't ride with me in my car alone. It's a boundary I've set up to protect my marriage. I don't want there ever to be an opportunity for something to happen or for someone else to see me together with a woman who is not my wife and wonder if something is going on between that person and me. To some, it may seem trivial, but for me, my marriage is far too important to risk it, so I set up boundaries to protect it.

Another boundary Robin and I have put in place is that we don't drink alcohol. Robin and I are totally abstinent from drinking. While we are not saying it's wrong for you, it's not something we do. This is a funny example of how situations can become cloudy very quickly. One Friday night, my wife and I were at Pancho Verde's Mexican restaurant.

We frequent that establishment quite regularly. We both enjoy the food and service immensely. That evening was no different than dozens of trips before. I had my usual virgin piña colada, and Robin followed suit and ordered one as well. Before the evening was up, we had drunk two or three of those and never thought anything of it. It's simply piña colada mix with no alcohol.

The following Sunday, we headed out to church, Union Hill Baptist Church, a little country church in the woods. We had been attending this church for about five years. I was head of our deacons, and I also served as chairperson of finance. It was a small church with a couple hundred attendees. When you go to a church that small, you have to wear multiple hats. A senior adult lady walked up to me just before the start of service and said, "With your position, I just want you to know that I'm very, very disappointed in you." I said, "Excuse me?" She said, "I was at Poncho Verde's, and sat in the corner, and I watched you and Robin get drunk." I said, "Oh, you did?" She said, "Yes, I did, and I'm very disappointed in you." I said, "I'm sorry; that will never happen again." I didn't explain it to her. I didn't tell her that they were virgin piña coladas, but I did tell Robin that night that we would never, ever again be seen in public drinking virgin piña coladas. If we're going to drink the mix, we're going to do it at home; we're not going to do it in public because it's perceived as something that it's not. In the mind of another, it's reality.

I could have told that lady all day long they were virgin piña coladas, and she would never have believed it. Now we have a boundary set in place for us so that misunderstanding never happens again. It's easy to think she should have been minding her own business, and I agree, she should have, but as a leader, there are greater expectations. We are and should be held to a higher degree of responsibility. It's the same thing as being a leader at work, in your community, or even in your home. You have to be very careful with the boundaries you set. You need to be sure you're influential in the right areas. You need to be careful where you go. You need to be careful what you say and who you're seen with at all times. I'm not saying it's wrong to be with any particular person or the other. It's just that you need to be mindful of it, and you can only do that if you predetermine your boundaries.

We have a few other boundaries that you also may want to consider for your family. If the entire family can't watch a movie on television or at the theater, we as adults don't look at it either. We stopped watching the news twelve years ago at the urging of my friend Dan Miller; it's proven to be great advice. If it's that important, someone will inform me. I can't handle shootings, stabbings, and murders just before bed. We allow no electronic devices at the dinner table—none. Leave your phone in the car on date night, or at least turn off the notifications.

There are no electronics, including television, in our bedroom. At premarriage counseling, our pastor told us that the bedroom was for two things: sleeping, and we would figure out the other. Watching television wasn't the second option. Robin has made our bedroom a sanctuary just for the two of us. There are no pictures of

...if you don't stand for something, you will fall for anything.

anyone but us, not even our children and grandchildren. Our bedroom, you could say, is off limits except for Robin and me. I will say that some of our boundaries are a bit extreme, but it works for us. I had rather everyone know where we take a stand because if you don't stand for something, you will fall for anything.

When Brooke and Hollie were young, I would say, "Make good decisions now rather than in the heat of the moment." It's the same in business. You have to predetermine that you're going to be ethical and moral, that you're going to be a person of character—even if it costs you time or money. Before your world collapses, why don't you make this commitment today? It seems odd to think that creating boundaries can give you an enormous amount of freedom because we're trained to believe just the opposite. When you have the right boundaries in place, you will find that you are freer than you've ever been without them.

LEAN IN . . .

- You need to make sure you align yourself with people who have high values and strong moral convictions and who have the same goals in life as you do.

- If we know the rules of the game to start with, there's going to be no hard feelings, but if we go into it (i.e., a partnership) with all these unanswered questions, there's a lot of room for conflict.

- Set personal and professional boundaries and enlist other people to hold you accountable to following each one.

- When you have the right boundaries in place, you will find that you are freer than you've ever been without them.

CHAPTER 6

BLINDSIDED

S ometimes life throws you curveballs when you least expect it. Your life may be going along perfectly, and all of a sudden, you are blindsided by a circumstance or an event that just literally rocks your world. That happened to me in 2001.

Things were going excellently. Our business was rocking and rolling; we were making money, and I had a schedule the world would envy. We had our plans in place, and everything was going just the way we wanted. On Wednesday mornings, I would go to our church and meet with our pastor and about a half dozen men for a time of prayer for our leadership and congregation. At this point in time, we had extraordinary momentum and unprecedented growth, adding about eighty to one hundred and twenty-five members per month. Long Hollow Baptist Church, at this time, was ranked as the fastest-growing Baptist church in the country. As an early riser, the half past five meeting time was a perfect fit. Normally, we would leave around seven.

Wednesday, August 1, 2001, was a hot and muggy day, very typical for Nashville that time of year, but this typical day was about to deal me a hand I was unprepared for. It started the same as most Wednesdays did, but it soon became a day that would change my life forever. I got up and went to church, as usual; the morning played out as normal. The pastor, myself, and the other men of the church met and prayed, and then I left to go to the office as I had done for years. I was driving down Gallatin Pike, a very busy, four-lane major highway connecting Hendersonville to Madison, where our business was located. I noticed there was a bus that had stopped on the right-hand side of the road— not at a bus stop, but in the middle of the right-hand lane.

I slowed down momentarily, looked to my left, and noticed a guy running across the two lanes of traffic that are northbound. He got to the center turning lane and hesitated. When he did, I let off the gas so I could decide if he was going to try to cross or if he was going to stay there. His shoulders slumped, and he went into a restful posture, so I sped back up.

Now, I'm doing about forty-five miles an hour because it's a major thoroughfare, and as soon as I get close to where the guy is standing, he takes off running for the bus as hard as he can go. And then it happened; I ran over a pedestrian. Actually, he hit me. He ran into the left front quarter panel of my Lincoln Navigator. When he hit the SUV, his head hit the driver-side mirror. It spun him around, and he hit the left rear quarter panel and fell face down in the middle of the road.

This all happened in a millisecond. I remember thinking, *God, what just happened?* I couldn't even fathom what had unfolded. It was like things slowed down to a crawl, and everything went into slow motion. I pulled over to the side of the road and stopped very quickly; I was shaking uncontrollably. I was thinking to myself, *God, please, no. Let this just be minor.* So many thoughts were racing through my mind. I grabbed my cell phone, jumped out of the car, and was paralyzed with fear. I turned and looked, and I saw the guy face down in the middle of the street, motionless. Cars were stopping abruptly everywhere. People were getting out of their vehicles and running to his aid. I couldn't get control of my shaking enough to dial 911 on my cell phone. I finally braced my right hand with my left, put my palms together, and I held my hand still enough to push 911.

I didn't know that other people were doing the same. In a matter of a few minutes, there were ambulances, police cars, fire trucks, and paramedics—you name it. All forms of emergency response vehicles were coming from everywhere. Traffic stopped both ways, and I was in a kind of shock. Even in the midst of total confusion, I don't re-member hearing the sirens. I walked over to where the guy was laying, and I saw that he was a senior adult male. I didn't know what to do, so I just stood there. When the ambulance arrived, two paramedics made repeated attempts to resuscitate, to no avail. It seemed like an eternity, but they worked with him for eight to ten minutes before loading him into the ambulance.

The police officer was very compassionate and genuinely interest-ed in my well-being. Very gently, he approached me, asked if I needed to call a friend or family member, and then instructed me to take a seat in his patrol car. Some other Metro police officers interviewed all bystanders, the bus driver, and another motorist. They quickly discov-ered that the testimony of everyone was the same: the gentleman just ran right out in front of me, and there was nothing I could have done differently. At the time this had no bearing on the way I felt. I had hit a pedestrian. My mind was racing with thoughts of his wife and chil-dren. Did he even have a family? Why did he attempt to catch the bus with so much traffic? Did I do something wrong? Was I paying enough attention, or was I speeding? I didn't know what to think or what to do next. I was afraid.

Three days later, I was contacted by the police department, and they told me the man I had hit had sustained severe head trauma and died within seventy-two hours of the accident.

When I think about how distracted drivers are today, it makes me nervous. You look around at every third car today, and the drivers are texting, sending an email, or surfing the web. I'm so thankful I wasn't doing something distracting. There are so many things that could have caused me not to see that man, but I wasn't distracted. I think it would have been even more difficult to deal with if I had not been paying attention. Please remember this the next time you are distracted while driving. It takes a nanosecond to miss something, and your entire life can change in an instant.

In this case, there was literally nothing I could have done to avoid the accident. He made the wrong decision. He just wasn't looking. We later discovered that he couldn't see well. His daughters and family had warned him that he shouldn't be out. The bus driver had warned him on multiple occasions to stop running out in front of traffic, and he just wouldn't listen.

Enrique was his name. He was from the Philippines, seventy-seven years old and in good health. He happened to be good friends with my personal physician, so he offered to call the family on my behalf. My doctor said, "Aaron and his family are honorable people. I'm certain it was an accident." To this day, I am very appreciative that he made that call. My attorney told me not to contact the man's family. However, I just couldn't allow myself not to contact them. Reaching out just seemed like the right thing to do, so regardless of the personal liabilities, I had to call. I waited several days before I contacted the family. I didn't want to go to the family. I didn't think that would be the right decision, but I at least wanted to talk to them and give my condolences.

When I called, Enrique's (last name not disclosed to protect the family) daughter answered. I paid my respects, and she said, "Mr. Walker, you have nothing to fear." I said, "I'm not worried about that. I'm not calling you because of litigation or any legal action; I'm calling you to give you my condolences." I felt sick to my stomach. I tried to prepare in my mind what I was going to say, but you can't prepare for telling someone you are sorry for such a tragedy. She thanked me profusely. She apologized for the fact that her mom didn't want to talk to me, but I understood that completely. To this day, I have yet to talk to his wife. Ironically, five years later when my dad was in an ICU, Enrique's daughter, the same one I spoke with, was my dad's nurse. What an unusual twist of events.

I was fortunate enough to have some close friends who stood in the gap for me and made themselves available for months. Robin was an absolute rock for me when I needed her most. She comforted me with every fiber of her being. She encouraged me to get professional help—counselors, coaches, or whatever I needed to work through this. A couple of my

During difficult times, we need others.

close friends, Greg Smith and Allen Lindsey, met with me for months over lunch and helped walk me through this. There was a local public figure here in Nashville who had had the same experience. He was kind enough to call me and give a word of encouragement. This is just one more reason that it's vital to have an inner circle of friends. During difficult times, we need others.

Therefore, encourage one another and build each other up, just as in fact you are doing.—*1 Thessalonians 5:11*

At this point, Robin and I pretty much made the decision we were going to sell the business. I just didn't want to be in business any longer. There was a lot of stress associated with the accident, as you can imagine. Several weeks later, I was back at the store working, wrestling with these decisions: What's next for us? What should we do? Should we continue working? The stress continued to mount as I dealt with these questions on a daily basis. I was trying to make the decision of selling my business or staying with it. I was forty years old at this point, and was thinking, *Do I just want to do more of the same, grind through, and persevere?* Let me be honest; hitting Enrique was the most horrific experience that I had ever encountered. I was managing employees and wrestling with how much is enough, all the while trying to find purpose in my life. I was a mess.

During this time frame, about a month after the accident, a customer walked up to me and laid some tools on the counter and made me an offer to buy them. I told him I couldn't sell them for his offer and thanked him. He persisted with ridiculous offers, and he was trying my patience. Honestly, I was not there mentally; I wasn't engaged with the client. I gave him another price, and he made a snide comment. By this time, I felt a tension welling up inside me, and I grabbed the tools in my hand, and I turned around and threw them towards the containers they had been in.

The guy said, "What are you doing?" I said, "Get out of here." He said, "I'm never coming back," and I said, "Good. I don't want you to come back. I don't even want to see you again." Something snapped in me. That had never happened to me before; I had never acted this way. I'm all about customer service, and this was totally out of character. My partner walked up to me, and said, "Big A, you okay?" I said, "No, I'm not; I'm not okay at all." He said, "Come on in the office." The store became eerily quiet. No one moved; it was like time stood still.

We were sitting in the office, and I was shaking uncontrollably. I was so upset. My guess is I was on the verge of a breakdown, but I don't know. I had never been in this frame of mind before, ever. I said, "I can't take this anymore." I just couldn't take the pressure of the decisions I was faced with. I made a conscience decision that moment that I was finished working. We agreed the next night to go to dinner together so we could talk about what to do next. I told him, "I want out. I want to sell it." Robin and I had decided to retire, again. I think it was a huge mistake. I was running *from* something rather than *to* something.

Herb and I met the next night at the Olive Garden restaurant near Rivergate Mall in Goodlettsville. I was sad, confused, and tired. We just sat there a few minutes, staring at each other; we were good enough friends that the silence was not awkward. "Robin and I are going to sell the business; I just want out." He loved me like a brother and said, "Not a problem." We had been together since 1974, and this was 2001, so we were like family. It took us ten minutes to reach an agreement. I told him the amount I wanted and the time frame I was willing to finance the purchase, and he agreed on the spot. Our attorney drafted the documents, and not thirty days later, I was gone. I was retired . . . again. I made so many mistakes in this process. I would never encourage someone to make such a major life decision under such duress. I should have taken at least six months to calm down emotionally, regroup, and seek the counsel of trained experts. If this happened today, I would handle it very differently. Make logical decisions, not emotional decisions.

August 1, 2001, without a question, changed my life forever. Through this process, I discovered we need to hold life very delicately because it's fragile. Before the accident, I thought I was invincible and bulletproof; I felt as though I could do anything, without many repercussions. I felt like I was going to live forever, but instead, I discovered that life can be taken away in an instant. We're not promised tomorrow; we should live every day to its fullest. We need to live today like it could be our last because it could be. I don't want to sound morbid, afraid, or frightened, but we never know what tomorrow brings. This experience highlighted for me just how precious our life is.

> We're not promised tomorrow; we should live every day to its fullest.

There were no immediate plans. I ended up taking off work for the next five years; I didn't do anything. We traveled extensively to places we had always wanted to visit. We took some cruises because we love the Caribbean, and we visited Alaska. I had to get away from the pain and the stress, and that was the way we chose to deal with it. I took a few trips to Canada and South America, fishing with a few close friends. I'm very thankful that we had the financial wherewithal to do this because it allowed me to heal. It allowed me to get away and not have to be confronted and deal with the emotions on a daily basis. We built a new house only a half mile from the house we raised Brooke and Hollie in. It was Hollie's senior year of high school, and Robin and I would soon be empty nesters. I guess building that house was part of the healing process for me. Another small piece of advice: don't build a house when you are trying to comfort yourself. You will spend way more than makes good business sense. The truth is, you should never make choices emotionally.

Why do we wait until something drastic or life altering happens before we make good choices? I want to emphasize in this book that we're intelligent people, and it doesn't have to take an accident for you to discover the true meaning and purpose of your life. We have to get a bad health report before we'll exercise or eat properly, or we'll have to go through a divorce before we turn our life around, or we'll have an accident like I did and then we sit up and take notice. Then the light comes on, and we discover there's more to life than thinking of ourselves. It was a very unfortunate circumstance, a very sad situation, even more so for Enrique and his family than for me, but as a direct result of it, I learned how to look at life differently. Ask yourself now, what are you taking for granted? Is it your spouse or maybe even your children? Are you slighting your relationships? I hope not; I hope you are fully engaged in the things that matter most.

The Lord is good, a stronghold in a day of distress; He cares for those who take refuge in Him.—Nahum 1:7 (HCSB)

That five-year break for me might have been unnecessary, but it allowed me to stop thinking about myself. Before the accident, I had fallen right back into my old mindset of thinking only about my desires and well-being. Every day, I was thinking about how I could scale my business or make just a little more money. "Things" were pretty important to me as well. Countless hours were dedicated to strategizing how I could build a nicer house, buy a vacation home, or drive a nicer car. Every single thought, every single day, revolved around me. I was looking inward all the time and never giving any consideration as to how I might help others. I wasn't a bad person; I was a pretty good guy. I think I was respected in the community, and my wife and I had a lot of close relationships, but I was all about myself. The accident brought clarity in many ways and created questions in others. If I believed that all talents come from God, how could I be so selfish just to use my skills in such a self-centered way?

Even the relationships that I'd formed were more about what I could get out of them than what I could offer. The money I made was meant for buying something nicer for myself. Every waking hour, I was figuring out how I could make Robin's life, my children's life, and my life better, with no thought whatsoever of other people.

We have different gifts, according to the grace given to each of us. If your gift is prophesying, then prophesy in accordance with your faith; if it is serving, then serve; if it is teaching, then teach; if it is to encourage, then give encouragement; if it is giving, then give generously; if it is to lead, do it diligently; if it is to show mercy, do it cheerfully.—Romans 12:6–8

What would my legacy be? Up until this point, all anyone could say about me was, "He came from humble beginnings; he made a little money; and was hyperfocused on his success. He was a pretty good golfer and a fair outdoorsman." Wow, what a legacy. Asking myself these questions was eye-opening. What would your legacy be?

At that time, nobody would have said his life was better as a result of having known me. Others would have all pointed to the tangible possessions I had, and if I were lucky, they would have commented on my outdoor skills. They would have looked to the life I had built for Robin and myself. They would have said, "What a fabulous house he had, and what incredible trips he took." But nobody would have said, "By knowing this guy, my life was better." At the realization of this, I was sad.

When I'm gone, I want people to be able to say I made a difference in their lives. I want to encourage, empower, and edify: "He encouraged, empowered, and edified me. He was always there for me; he helped me during my trials; he inspired me to make my life better." I want a significant life, one that truly matters, not necessarily just a successful one.

During this five-year break, I started going to a very good mentor/coach, and I learned that I'm a creator/developer, not a maintainer/manager. Nothing will keep my enthusiasm if there's not a challenge; no amount of money will ever keep my interest if there is not opportunity before me. The question then became, "How can I use being a creator/developer not only to be successful personally, but also to breathe life into other people? What can I do to be of assistance to them? How can I be significant and live a purposeful life, both personally and professionally? What can I do to help other people, all while making a living?"

Another discovery was the limited time I had spent on personal development. Having this much free time allowed me to read more, study, and meditate. Being a hard charger, sleep was not high on my priority list, but during this down time, I discovered the value of rest. We are all more inclined to make good decisions when well rested.

I would like you to take a personal assessment of yourself: What is your motivation? What are your ideals? What is your identity tied to? Look at your career, your personal relationships, your faith, and the people around you. What are you doing to be significant in the lives of other people? Or are you completely focused inward, making it all about you? During this break, I was able to do a personal assessment and found myself a better person overall because I was willing to do what was necessary to change my life and become the person I was called to be—instead of the person I was pretending to be.

One of the biggest things I realized through this part of my life is that there are no blanket statements that say this is what being success-ful is, or this is what significance looks like. Success and significance can be different for each person. You have to make that decision for yourself, and you do that by assessing every angle of your life and de-ciding what's important to you.

For me, the most significant thing in my life is my relationship with Christ; everything stems and flows out of that. The second most significant area of my life is my family. I want to be there for my wife and my children. These days are fun because my five grandchildren fill the majority of my time. The other relationships in my life come third and then financial security after that. Putting an order to the most sig-nificant parts of your life will help you to always stay focused on what's most important. If you get any of those out of order, it can put a strain on how significant you will become in the misplaced area. For instance, if you put other relationships ahead of your family, then there will be problems down the road.

You will have to assess your life and list out the most important areas to focus on going forward. It took a horrendous accident and a five-year break for me to discover the value of putting things in the right order: faith, family, relationships, and then financial security. Be proactive in your life now and never let it get to that point before you decide to figure out your strategy to be significant.

One additional lesson learned was how to remain content while never giving in to complacency. Complacency happens when you get to a point that you're done trying to make things better. You accept things as they are and take on a "whatever . . . can't do anything about it anyway" attitude. Contentment is accepting things in life as they are and knowing they are

...complacency is the same as giving up.

truly good, but still having the desire to make them better if you can. I never want to be complacent. For me, complacency is the same as giving up. We can, however, learn to be content in all situations. Take some time to enjoy today and fully engage each moment that life brings you because this moment is going to be over in a little while, and you will never get it back; ask yourself if you truly gave it the justice it deserved. If you don't fully engage in the moment, you'll never truly learn to be content.

Not that I speak in respect of want: for I have learned, in whatsoever state I am, therewith to be content. I know both how to be abased, and I know how to abound: every where and in all things I am instructed both to be full and to be hungry, both to abound and to suffer need. I can do all things through Christ which strengtheneth me.— Philippians 4:11–13 (KJV)

Everyone matters. Engaging fully with a loyal friend or family member in a deep, heartfelt conversation is invaluable. When you block out all the distractions, make eye contact, and sincerely show interest, your relationships will go to levels not yet experienced. In today's fast-paced world, we have lost the ability to do that. Focus on the person you are conversing with and give the conversation all of your attention. We've all been with people before, having a conversation but they're tweeting, emailing, calling, or texting with someone else. I always want to say, "Hello! I'm talking to you. What are you doing?" We do this with our spouses, our children, and friends. We want to know why our children don't pay attention to us. Stop for a moment and see how engaged you are with them. They deserve your full attention.

Robin recently called me out on taking so many pictures. She said, "Can't we just enjoy the moment?" By the time we all get ready for the photo, we miss the moment. I'm guilty of wanting to share the shot on social media, with many people I don't even know. I want everybody to see what an excellent time I'm having, rather than enjoying the moment. Why don't we fully engage at that moment and learn to be content with where we are right then? Many times, in marriage, it's quite romantic to share in something that only the two of you are involved with; this is how memories are created.

It is virtually impossible to describe all the life lessons I learned as a direct result of the accident. In summary, it taught me to enjoy whomever I'm with, wherever I'm at, and to live in that moment. God has gifted all of us with multiple talents, wonderful experiences, and phenomenal relationships. Don't miss it!

This is the day which the LORD hath made; we will rejoice and be glad in it.— Psalm 118:24 (KJV)

LEAN IN . . .

■ Your life may be going along perfectly, and all of a sudden, you are blindsided by a circumstance or an event that just literally rocks your world.

■ It takes a nanosecond to miss something, and your entire life can change in an instant.

■ Make logical decisions, not emotional decisions.

■ Discover the value of rest. We are all more inclined to make good decisions when well rested.

■ If you don't fully engage in the moment, you'll never truly learn to be content.

CHAPTER 7

THE EAGLES

There are some things in life that don't matter, and then there are other things that we all wish we had discovered earlier. As a speaker, I regularly get asked, "What would you have done earlier in your career if you had another opportunity?" I believe this is one of the best questions you could ask anyone who has had any measure of success. Hands down, unequivocally, with no hesitation, I would have joined a great mastermind at the very start of my journey. Masterminding is something that has been instrumental in my quest to a view from the top. I consider this a foundational block for my success. While I talked about masterminding earlier in the book, it was only briefly, and I feel a real need to devote a little more time to unpacking some of its benefits since it's played such a vital role in my life.

A mastermind group means different things to different people. It is the coordination of knowledge and effort of two or more individuals who work toward a definite purpose in the spirit of harmony.

For lack of guidance a nation falls, but victory is won through many advisors.—Proverbs 11:14

Many years ago, I was recruited by Dave Ramsey to be part of a mastermind called the Eagles. It was originally a Bible study with Ron Doyle, Dan Miller, and Dave Ramsey, but when the Bible study was over, none of them wanted to stop meeting. The study was very intentional and created by a company called CLC (Christian Leadership Concepts), of which Ron Doyle was executive director. Founded here in Nashville, it's a two-year program that brings men together on a weekly basis, studying Scripture, reading books, and often praying together. They decided at the conclusion to transform it into a mastermind, to soar to heights like never before, thus the name, the Eagles. Dave, Ron, and Dan were all responsible for enlisting a couple of guys each to join and start this group.

The only real requirement to participate in the group was that you were an honest man of good character. It didn't hurt me any that I was a guest of Dave. The foundation was formed with high moral values, not on your financial statement. There were no restrictions based on the type of business or your position in the community. The litmus test was if you were interested in investing in long-term relationships to spur you on to higher achievements. The Eagles were going to be made up of level-five leaders with high integrity.

To show our sincerity, we chose to sign an annual commitment to participate. They wanted each guy in the group to have a point in time that he was able to get out of the mastermind, or he could renew annually. The agreement was pretty stringent. It clearly defined what was expected of each member. If we were not sick or out of town, we committed to be there. Meeting was not something that we wanted to do haphazardly; we wanted true commitment. We met at Dave's office at seven o'clock on Wednesday mornings. Each person needed to be there to participate because it wasn't fair to the guys who got up early and showed up not to have the value added by each participant. It was a refreshing commitment to make, to not only verbalize but also to put in writing that you would be actively involved.

Dave has an excellent conference room, perfect for this type of meeting, which is adjacent to his personal office. He graciously offered it up for our use every week. We would meet for about an hour and a half every week unless something serious prolonged the meeting. We didn't want guys in there who were going to sit in the corner like a sponge and just take and take and take; you had to give too. It is of no benefit for anyone to sit idly by and not offer up his vantage point. We had a room full of highly opinionated men, and I'm thankful for every single one of them.

There was a little bit of a format, but it wasn't highly structured. If you were the first one there, you were expected to get the coffee going; you can't have a great meeting without a pot of java. Everyone had keys to Dave's office, so we would just go in when we got there. I'd make coffee and turn on the lights and hang out with the other early birds, like Jeff Mosley and Don Scurlock. Historically, men have to have something to focus on, or we will chase rabbits. At any moment, we could find ourselves talking about basketball, football, deer hunting, and a host of other interests. Therefore, to keep ourselves focused on one topic, we chose to read books and discuss them in depth.

We read hundreds of books over the course of our time together, and each week one of the guys would volunteer to facilitate the discussion. Before we left, we would assign a couple of chapters, and one of us would volunteer to lead the following week.

There were a couple of very rare instances when men would need to leave the group because of personal or professional reasons, and someone would suggest another remarkable man, trying to keep the team to ten to twelve guys. It was decided early on that it would have to be a unanimous vote to allow someone new in.

Being part of a mastermind is about people raising the bar. Within this group of men, we were always trying to challenge and encourage one another. I loved to tease and banter back and forth with these guys; they all had such a great sense of humor. You know how it is with a bunch of guys with strong personalities; we are always striving for position, in a fun way. You get in a room full of a bunch of alpha males, guys who are go-getters, and they will challenge each other. The good and the bad about this group was their incredible memories. If you spoke it, they didn't forget it, and they always were checking in on your progress. I didn't want to go the following week and not have done my task or the things that these guys had challenged me to do, so we were always helping each other raise our individual bars.

Having that support also helps you create and implement goals. These guys were strategic thinkers by nature and helped me figure out things I didn't see. That was one of the group's qualities that was vital to me—creativity. When you're left to yourself, you can only see something your way. But when you put yourself in a group of guys who you know are honest and credible, who have high integrity and want the best for you, you can trust their creative input. They can say, "Hey, have you thought about doing it this way? Or have you looked at it from this perspective?"

Everyone in the mastermind was in a different profession. They also were raised differently and came from different parts of the country. Each looked at life through a distinct filter or lens. And the group benefited from having access to all these different views of a problem or issue. It was just very encouraging to me to be in a room full of such diverse guys. You don't know what you don't know, and every time you shared something, someone else would have a different perspective.

To be honest with you, sometimes I didn't like their ideas, but the more I thought about them, the more buy-in I got from the other guys, and the more I trusted their consensus, I realized they actually formulated some great ways to do things. The value of brainstorming with each other is immeasurable, just sitting together at a table and kicking ideas around. It was fun; we could dream big with no consequences. Sometimes I was embarrassed because what seemed like a superb idea in my mind proved to be insane after an hour discussion. Oh, well, I had rather have looked foolish in there as opposed to losing a fortune and revealing my stupidity to the world.

In a mastermind, you can share your grandiose ideas and dream in a spectacular way, yet never leave your seat. You have the support of each person. Each has agreed to be totally honest with you in a very respectful way. You've got people who are not afraid to say, "You know, practically speaking, that's just not going to work." Or, "If you implement this strategy piece by piece, step by step, and apply it consistently, this just might work." Through this process, a lot of brainstorming ideas would come to fruition and pay big dividends.

The value of brainstorming with each other is immeasurable...

Masterminding allows you to tap into the experience of everyone in the group. Many of these guys had twenty-plus years in their respective careers. The value of that diverse knowledge was especially clear when one of us wanted to step outside his comfort zone and tackle a new project. Someone was always able to step up to the plate and offer incredibly valuable and often hard-won wisdom, whatever the project encompassed.

Let each of you look not only to his own interests but also to the interests of others.—Philippians 2:4 (ESV)

You gain a lot of confidence by being around others with similar aspirations. When you are in a room by yourself, you hear these voices: *How can I do this? I'm not sure I can.* There's no encouragement there; there's nothing to help build your confidence. But when you are in a committed group, they can help dispel the doubt.

Your unbiased, personal board of directors is how I describe a mastermind group. If you get guys around the table who have something to gain or lose by what they are trying to offer or share, you might not get an honest opinion. But when they are unbiased and don't have anything to gain or lose, they can be your true advocate. They end up being allies who are a boost to your everyday positive mental attitude. After years and years of meeting with the same group, you develop a sense of trust that is hard to describe. There's a feeling of security because you know you have an excellent team you can count on regularly. There were times I came into the group feeling lost and discouraged. These guys helped me to overcome these feelings of helplessness and anxiety. They will help you work through it, and they might give you a resource, connection, or direction on the next best steps.

More than anything, the value of accountability in a mastermind makes it worth the effort. Have you ever wanted to do something so badly but you could not muster up the mojo to complete it? I know I can raise my hand high on this one. Before joining this group, I was excellent coming out of the gate, an impressive self-starter, but a lousy finisher. There's a sense of motivation that we all have, but time slips by. Other priorities appear, and the next thing I realize is that all my important tasks are way down the list. Motivation is an exhaustible resource, and you can't stay hyped-up indefinitely. A written plan is good and needed, but when you have five or ten people each week asking if you got something accomplished, you tend to pay a lot more attention. You can achieve your goals much faster by having that accountability.

> More than anything, the value of accountability in a mastermind makes it worth the effort.

There were a lot of guys in my group who had great businesses and larger companies than mine. I have to admit that at first I was a little intimidated. After spending time with these guys, however, that feeling dissipated. I soon came to the realization that there would always be guys ahead of me, no matter the level I was at presently. I could use this to my advantage once I was able to tame my pride. When you surround yourself with others who possess wisdom and experience, you will always be better off as a direct result of their life lessons. It's cheaper to learn on their dime.

One pleasant surprise to me was the level of encouragement I received. The group would show me ways to do so many things such as add more employees, add more locations, or spend more time, effort, and energy on certain tasks that I wasn't necessarily good at. They helped me understand that if there was an area I wasn't gifted in, I could delegate it away or learn a better process. They were always nudging me along to take it to the next level, to take that next step. They helped me figure out how to do it a better way.

The diversity of the mastermind members is sometimes misunderstood. If everybody was just like you, you wouldn't need anybody else—just you. Being like-minded regarding advancing is good, but varying views are welcomed to allow new perspectives.

I am very thankful that the Eagles weren't just focused on business. There were, and always will be, difficult family situations that needed our undivided attention. Multiple times I went to the group with disturbing news or problem areas in my marriage or with our children for which I needed wisdom to make a decision. Every man in the room at one time or the other was confronted with situations like these. I had been married probably as long or longer than anybody in the group, so while I might not have had some of the business experience some of them had, I had life experience that many of them did not. Robin and I were married at a very early age; I was nineteen, and she was eighteen, just two weeks out of school. We had children just three years later, and this gave me a huge head start over most of the guys. I was outranked in some of the business discussions, but on the family front, I was often called front and center. I didn't always make the right decision, so these guys wanted to learn on my dime.

It seemed as though our marriages were always being discussed. When you are a small business owner and entrepreneur, and all of us were, there is always trouble lurking in the shadows. I can't say that any of us were at any time in grave danger—well, maybe close—but I can say we had issues from time to time. One of the big hang-ups for Robin and me is work/life balance. I've always thought that as long as I am awake, opportunity is knocking. I wasn't that bad, but I have always worked a lot. We only argued over the amount I worked—and the thermostat, but that's another story.

All the Eagles at one time or another shared similar struggles. Everyone except Ron Doyle; he always seemed to have a good handle on when to stop working. A day did come when I had to make some pretty severe cuts to my schedule to keep peace in the family. Looking back, I would have been better served by making these adjustments earlier. Robin would often send up a warning shot and say, "Don't make a lot of money at the expense of our relationship," and she was right.

Teenage years with the children added gray hair, and in-laws caused havoc often. Someone in the mastermind had just gone through these issues or was about to.

My point in sharing a few of these challenges is to let you know that you are not alone. No matter what your position in life, regardless of your status, no matter how much cash you have, we all have problems.

The salvation to all these is that you do not have to do it alone. There are beautiful people all around you. You may not realize that, and it could be because you have not been looking for them. Just a sidebar, we frequently find what we look for, good or bad. A mastermind that operates properly can save you from severe pain. If it didn't, I would not have participated in them now for more than twenty years.

Being a great husband and father is a monumental task, to say the least. Couple that with striving to be a rock star business person, and you are confronted with stress beyond measure. When you have these many plates spinning, it's exhausting doing it alone. One of the biggest encouragements and life lessons that I have learned from being involved in the mastermind is this: be present at home when you're present. We would be kidding ourselves, and those around us, if we said this challenge was a nonissue; we all struggle in this area. The truth is we are too busy; we just want to accomplish too much, too quickly. Having this group allowed me a place to vent. When I think back, I can't imagine what might have happened in my marriage had I not been surrounded by guys who wanted the best for me and my life.

We even had subsets, not intentionally, just guys who connected alone to talk through a situation and spend more time burrowing in and digging deeper. Tommy Summers and Don Scurlock were two guys that I had lunch with regularly because we had similar interests. Relationships happen when you spend quality time with one another. Tommy and I had real estate and stocks to discuss, and Don and I love the outdoors.

Events happen over the course of your life that require more than an hour-long meeting. I had situations, and the others did as well, that called for additional time. When it was something that was very challenging that didn't require the entire group, one or two guys who knew you best would get you off to the side or take you to lunch and talk through things that were serious in nature. Meeting for a dozen plus years, you go through a lot. What is so fantastic about investing in others, and them in you, is the bar continually gets raised. I loved the challenge. It made me a better man.

> Masterminding can create relationships like you've never experienced before

Masterminding can create relationships like you've never experienced before. As guys, we aren't taught to share, but when you spend that much time with guys, week after week, you get to know them very intimately, and there is a passion that wells up in you to serve one another. The sooner you can let the public perception go and eliminate the facade, the sooner you are willing to subject yourself to the scrutiny of others. Once you are prepared to listen, you will get to a spot of incredible strength because there is great power in that type of humility. The truth is, we all have areas that we are weak in; there is not a person living who has every area of his life mastered. Some people are adamant at work and vulnerable at home. Other guys spend way too much time at home and need to get into the workplace.

There's a tension we all feel, regardless of where we are in life. It's that work/life pressure. You need to embrace that pressure because it keeps you in the center of the road, and that is what we did in these relationships. That pressure is what keeps you focused on your decisions. We would encourage one another to evaluate regularly. Balance is hard to achieve for anyone, so I would urge you to pick the correct areas of life to focus on for your family and devote the necessary energy to be successful there. At different seasons in your life, your focus will be different, so adjust the balance. Don't ever feel your decisions for today are etched in stone. Be willing to pivot or change. Communication with your family and advisors is crucial. You may believe this to be good news, or possibly bad news; you will have to decide, but the tension never leaves, regardless of your position in life. Your money, status, or age never eliminate this feeling. Managing the decisions and trusting the council of the multitudes is your best option. The good news is that in a mastermind, like the one I have had the privilege of experiencing, there are people there to help you.

As I'm writing this, I'm sitting on my patio, very early on a Saturday morning. My house is in the middle of the woods, and I feel very blessed to enjoy watching the deer, birds, and turkey. The simple pleasures of life are very rewarding. I get the same sense of gratitude when I think about my group of guys, the Eagles. I'm encouraged I have fostered long-term relationships that allow me to share trials, challenges, and victories and not be seen any differently, regardless of who I am that day.

LEAN IN . . .

- When you're left to yourself, you can only see something your way. But when you put yourself in a group of guys who you know are honest and credible, who have high integrity and want the best for you, you can trust their creative input.

- There's a sense of motivation that we all have, but time slips by. Other priorities appear, and the next thing I realize is that all my important tasks are way down the list. Motivation is an exhaustible resource, and you can't stay hyped-up indefinitely.

- When you surround yourself with others who possess wisdom and experience, you will always be better off as a direct result of their life lessons.

- The diversity of the mastermind members is sometimes misunderstood. If everybody was just like you, you wouldn't need anybody else.

- There's a tension we all feel, regardless of where we are in life. It's that work/life pressure. You need to embrace that pressure because it keeps you in the center of the road, and that is what we did in these relationships. That pressure is what keeps you focused on your decisions.

CHAPTER 8

IRON SHARPENS IRON

There was a time in my life that was very dark. I had personal and professional challenges like I had never experienced. I couldn't shake them. I listened to the voices in my head telling me it was never going to get better. I thought my life was going to suck forever. Have you ever been stuck? I was in the ditch; it felt like a grave with both ends kicked out. No matter which way I turned, it felt wrong. When you are going it alone, you will stay in the rut longer; that's just the way it is. When you are in a community, there is always an extended hand to grab that will pull you to safety.

If one person in our mastermind was in an atrocious spot, he dominated the time until we got it resolved. My issues went on for months, not because they couldn't be resolved but because I wouldn't let them go. I just kept saying, "I don't know what to do. This situation is what I'm dealing with, and it's difficult." I was whining, and I got to the point where I would begin to feel embarrassed about my behavior. During one of my extended rants one Wednesday, Dan looked over his glasses at me and then at Dave. It made me angry because I felt this was insensitive and disrespectful. It was the beginning of the end. I was on my way to recovery; I just did not know it yet. All of these guys had the guts to call you out and push you forward. I was mad at the time; now, I want to hug them.

One Saturday morning I was at ACE Hardware, and I got a phone call from mastermind member James Ryle. James was a respected national speaker, noted author, and probably one of the best storytellers on the planet. Now, keep in mind that we rarely talked to each other on the weekends. We tried to respect everyone's time with his family, so when I saw a call coming in, I knew it was going to be good or appalling. I didn't know which. I wasn't prepared for what was ahead. I answered the phone, and he asked if I had a minute. I walked outside where it was quiet. He said, "Brother, are you doing good?" I told him things were okay. He said, "I was praying for you this morning, and God gave me a word for you."

I thought, *Well, this is James Ryle, a highly respected individual and really great guy, commissioned to bring me a word from God. Wow! He has been through trials of his own and has a fascinating background.* I was processing this in my brain, thinking this was almost divine intervention from the Holy Spirit. I thought, *This is going to be so powerful!* I was excited. I thought, *Finally, somebody's going to give me something that's going to help me.* He said, "Are you ready?" Of course I was! I was anxious and excited to hear his words of wisdom. Then it happened. He said, "You're worrying the hell out of everybody in our group." I just started laughing. I said, "No, really, what is it?" He continued, "We are sick and tired of hearing you whining and complaining and going on and on. This morning I was reading Isaiah 52:1–2.

Awake, awake, Zion, clothe yourself with strength! Put on your garments of splendor, Jerusalem, the holy city. The uncircumcised and defiled will not enter you again. Shake off your dust; Rise up, sit enthroned, Jerusalem. Free yourself from the chains on your neck, Daughter Zion, now a captive.—Isaiah 52:1–2

"Aaron, it's time to take the chains from around your neck and move on. Brother, it's time you were moving on from this." Then he told me he had to go and hung up. I was standing there thinking, *What audacity!* James ruined my Saturday. He upset me beyond description, and I was so aggravated. I stood there clutching the phone in my hand and couldn't even fathom how he had the nerve to call me out like this.

After the initial shock, I thought it through for a few minutes. This guy had spent a decade with me, and he loved me enough to call me and tell me the truth. His call was like somebody pushed me off a cliff. And guess what? From that moment on, I was able to move forward. He was right. He pointed me back to Scriptures that said, "It's time; it's time we get over some things that are holding us down. We are captives in our minds. We don't see a way out, and it hinders us from living a life of excellence."

For me, that was a defining moment in my personal life. I needed somebody to come up and shake me because, apparently, them just telling me what I needed to consider doing wasn't working. With my personality, I needed someone to sucker punch me, and he did. I had to take responsibility and let my ego go. He got my attention. I apologized to the group. They helped me work through it, and I moved on.

If you're unwilling to listen to the Jameses of the world, don't get into a mastermind. If you're not willing to be blatantly honest with your peers and share the truth, stay away from accountability groups and masterminds. The world is full of do-gooders and surface-level friends; what we need are allies willing to speak truth into our life, who have the courage to stand alone and tell the truth. Don't survey the room and gather a consensus before sharing your thoughts. There have been many times I have been the chairman of committees, and people would come up to me outside the board meeting and say they wanted to talk about a controversial topic. I would say, "No way we are discussing this here and now. You're not talking to me about that now because you need to say that in the meeting; out here, nobody can fix it, but in the conference, resolution can be found. In the parking lot, it's merely gossip." It's the same way in a mastermind. These guys wouldn't go behind your back and talk about you and not be able to come and say it directly to your face.

> **If you're not willing to be blatantly honest with your peers and share the truth, stay away from accountability groups and masterminds.**

Pride goeth before destruction, and a haughty spirit before a fall.—Proverbs 16:18 (KJV)

We are all people of the flesh, so we're going to make mistakes sometimes. If somebody started heading down a trail about something that could be perceived as gossip, someone in the group would quickly cut that off. I remember a particular situation where one of the guys in the group wasn't there and somebody brought up something about his situation, and David Foster got up. He physically stood up and pointed his finger at the center of the conference room table and said, "Wait a minute. He's not here to defend that, and we are not talking about him when he's not here." And he was 100 percent right. Every group has to have courageous people who are willing to stand up and call you out.

It is necessary to have others' best interest at heart at all times. It's not for a coffee club, a social outing, or a gossip corner that we come together each week. A mastermind is to help each other, to encourage each other, to be honest and forthcoming.

We had times when we affirmed each other. This was done on a yearly basis, away from the office meeting space. Each person would take a turn and talk about how a specific person had impacted him. We would say things like the following: "You may not realize it, but you encouraged me in a particular area"; "Thanks for calling me out when I needed to hear it"; "The resource you gave me and these connections you created for me made a huge difference in my life." Each of us in the group took a turn affirming each other in that way. It was very emotional and meaningful.

Men need affirmation, and quite honestly, it was very uncomfortable for me the first couple of times we did that because it was something I hadn't ever done. I had never affirmed anyone in front of somebody else. I had patted someone on the back and said thank you or I appreciate that, but it was different to sit and look at another adult male and say, "I can't even begin to tell you the impact that you've had on my life personally, and I can't thank you enough for introducing me to this person (or for that resource or for those words of encouragement).” I was able to look at James Ryle in the eye and thank him for calling me out and telling me how much I was worrying everybody. I was able to let him know how much he changed my life as a result of that conversation.

It's indescribable what transpires through the years when you develop these types of relationships. It's not just a meeting. At this point, you're doing life together. You see each other outside the group. You vacation together. You've always got each other's back. As an example, I was at an event where there was a speaker. He called out one of the members of our group by name from on stage. I was furious because the speaker did not have a clue what he was talking about. He was talking about my friend, and what he was saying was inaccurate. I texted my fellow mastermind member immediately and said, “I want you to know that this guy is not in your corner. He's talking pretty negatively about you on stage.” You build this Marine mentality where you always have each other's backs, to help and support each other. It's like family; you don't allow people to talk about them negatively without being there to defend themselves. The camaraderie is beyond description because these people become a part of your extended family, and they are a significant part of your life.

Masterminds can start and they can stop, but that doesn't at all mean you will dismantle those lifelong relationships. When you share births, graduations, deaths, weddings, funerals, and holidays, it's permanent. One of our members' dad died unexpectedly. I got a phone call from Dave, saying we needed to go to the funeral—but it was in Kansas City, and we were in Nashville. Dave said not to worry about it and just to meet him at the airport. We got there, and he had a Lear jet ready to take us. I know everyone can't take a plane to a funeral. This is a very unusual and an exaggerated scenario, totally out of the norm for most people, but I'm just trying to impress upon you the depth of our relationships. When you genuinely care about others, you do unusual stuff.

When we walked in unexpectedly, my friend broke into a huge smile and peace came over his face. He said, "When I looked up and saw you all walk in, I knew everything was going to be okay because my guys are here." We had those kind of life experiences. I know when my dad died in 2006, these same men came pouring in

> When you genuinely care about others, you do unusual stuff.

and patiently waited over two hours to see me. It's just those real-life situations that you have to experience to understand how impactful they are. The caring, the genuineness, the outpouring of love and respect are immeasurable.

In the early years, we always prefaced our comments with, "This is private; don't tell anyone." As time went on, we just said what we had to say, with no precursor. In the early days of our mastermind meetings, we would say, "Tell me the truth. Just be honest with me." But it went without saying as we moved forward in our relationships because these guys were going to tell you the truth, regardless of the cost, because they loved you and they wanted the best for you and wanted to help you. When you are totally transparent and people tell you the truth, you get where you want to go much faster. You are just a little banged up when you get there.

I've taken a lot of time here to elaborate on the importance of masterminds. My life has been forever changed because of this group of guys. What would be the downside? Who would not want a band of brothers? Who would not want people to tell him the truth? Who would not want the encouragement, the edification, and the empowerment of people offering that word of caution?

Don't shield yourself and hide behind a curtain. Living a life of lies is exhausting. If you are not sharing life with someone, you have a difficult path ahead of you. A mastermind group can radically change your life—if you're willing.

Your business may survive on your own experience, but it will not perform to the level it could have if you had a tight inner circle of advisors. With a mastermind, you will always be raising the bar by tapping into the experience of others. You'll gain confidence by being around those with similar aspirations. It's a boost to your everyday positive mental attitude. When you build that kind of relationship with guys, then it becomes easier to share, trust, and accept feedback and criticism because "iron sharpens iron."

As iron sharpens iron, so one person sharpens another.—Proverbs 27:17

LEAN IN . . .

- When you are going it alone, you will stay in the rut longer; that's just the way it is. By being in a community, there is always an extended hand to grab that will pull you to safety.

- It's time we get over some things that are holding us down. We are captives in our minds. We don't see a way out, and it hinders us from living a life of excellence.

- The world is full of do-gooders and surface-level friends; what we need are allies willing to speak truth into our life, who have the courage to stand alone and tell the truth.

- When you are totally transparent and people tell you the truth, you get where you want to go much faster.

- Don't shield yourself and hide behind a curtain. Living a life of lies is exhausting. If you are not sharing life with someone, you have a difficult path ahead of you. A mastermind group can radically change your life—if you're willing.

CHAPTER 9
FOCUS

strive to do a great job, and then I take a break. I reengage and give it all I have once again, and then I take another break; it was becoming a habit in my life. I'm an all-in kind of guy, and then I rest, regroup, and start something else. Historically, your forties and fifties are the most productive time of your life financially, but I had done well early on in my twenties. I was not that good—I just started young, and I mean *really* young. After that first stint of nine years, I was twenty-seven years old. I took an eighteen-month sabbatical and then worked like no other for ten years, in another brick and mortar business. Then I took a break again, for five years.

There were two contributing factors in that extended five-year break. One was I was just tired, and the other was I had that life-changing accident, and I just needed time to recover. Those two things coupled together caused me to take a longer break than I should have. Once again, it was my wife who woke me up. She told me I was getting on her nerves, and I had to do something. Sitting around the house was not serving me well. While I was playing golf or fishing, my buddies were out making a living; they were building a legacy, and doing extremely well financially. And there I was just doing nothing.

Work hard and do not be lazy.—Romans 12:11a (GNT)

Robin and I had built a new house during this extended break; it took about a year and a half. I was a general contractor's nightmare because I was there every single day, all day long. I loved watching the progress of something develop. Remember, I'm a creator/developer, so I enjoy the process. Plus, it was my house, and that made it twice as enjoyable.

At the end of the project, I started thinking about how much I loved being part of building the house. I had a crazy thought: *What if I got into custom home building? Would I be any good at it? Could I make a living doing this?* I wasn't interested in the actual building part; I was interested in building a new business. It has always been the art of the deal for me. I didn't have any skills for physically building a home, but I did have business know-how. I knew I could help the guy who built my house with the business side of things—such as the development, marketing, and promotions. He was a small builder; he only built one or two houses a year. He had no employees, no office, no phone. You couldn't even get in touch with him because there wasn't even a listing for him. His marketing strategy was simply word-of-mouth. He was a master craftsman and had a reputation of being phenomenal. His name was David Patton, founder of David Patton Construction and one of the greatest guys I have ever known. David would sacrifice his well-being for your benefit. There never will be a better craftsman; David is one of a kind.

I approached him one day and said, "Why don't we take your talents and my resources and experience and join forces and create a custom home business like no other?" He explained he didn't have any experience in partnerships at all. I told him, "You just do what you do, and I'll take care of the rest." So, he thought about it, prayed about it, talked it over with family and friends, and decided to go for it.

I owned an office building in Goodlettsville, Tennessee, that I leased out to a company called Giant Photos. I went to them and offered to lower their rent if I could use the upstairs portion of the building, which was about 1,600 square feet. They happily agreed to those terms; they were not even using that part of the building. It was a win-win for everyone. We completely renovated the top floor and made it a state-of-the-art suite of offices, complete with a reception area, five offices, and a beautiful conference room. It had an exterior entrance, and it made an incredible place to work from when it was finished. We started operating out of that location and grew very rapidly. David continued to man the field, and I started attending trade shows and developed a marketing plan, which got me heavily involved in the local community. For a second time in my career, I started advertising on Dave Ramsey's show, promoting to high-end residents. When you focus all your efforts in a concentrated

...you need to choose your area of expertise wisely and do it very deliberately.

fashion with a well-thought-out plan, success happens. According to a local publication, we became the people's choice three consecutive years over an eight-year period.

I learned another valuable lesson through this process: you need to choose your area of expertise wisely and do it very deliberately.

My giftedness was growing businesses; David's talent was building. The construction industry had its unique intricacies that I had not encountered in the other brick and mortar businesses I had run. There were just a lot of things that went along with construction that I was unaware of in the beginning. While not necessarily bad, they were just different. I discovered a few years later that while some of my skills were needed and used, there were areas of the business in which I struggled and felt unprepared to deal with.

As I developed the strategy for the business, I found myself alone the majority of the time. That was a real negative for me since I love people. Unbeknownst to me, this was having a negative impact on my personality. Isolation is an enemy of excellence. When you own a high-end residential building company, you don't have that many clients. I was starving for the relationship side of things, as I feel like God has uniquely gifted me to interact with people. I love engaging with people, and as a result of limited exposure to others, I quickly became bored. Our plan was working, and we were succeeding in growing the business, but there were just dynamics that didn't fit who I am.

I didn't take the time to research that industry to see if it was something I would be equipped for; the partnership had just seemed like a good idea at the time. There's no way I would have gone into that business if I had taken the time to research it properly, like I knew how to do. I made the decision out of haste because I was feeling less than purposeful. I should have checked into other opportunities, and it was done on almost a whim because I was experiencing guilt for not working at all. I hate to admit that, but it's true. I saw an opportunity to partner with someone who had great skills, perfect character, and was honest to a fault. It was his unique giftedness. It was where he was supposed to be, but it was, without a doubt, not where I belonged.

Each one should use whatever gift he has received to serve others, faithfully administering God's grace in its various forms.—
1 Peter 4:10

Fundamentally, businesses are the same regarding how they operate, but they are also each uniquely different. I discovered that the construction industry is a very emotional business. When someone is making a new home purchase, it's the largest investment he is going to make, so it's his baby. It's not like buying a diamond ring or a new car; this is his house. He is going to live in it, raise his children in it, and possibly retire there. Building a house is a big-deal purchase. It's got to be perfect and exactly what he wants. For me, building our house wasn't as much emotional as it was strategic and financial, so I wasn't prepared for that.

When building a midlevel house, say for $300,000, it's handled much differently than a multimillion-dollar house. For a higher-end residence, there are tremendous demands. This clientele is accustomed to the finest, with no limitations and few boundaries, if any. Therefore, it takes twice as long to build their homes because they can't make a decision. When the world is your playground and you can have most anything you want, there is always a fear of selecting the wrong thing. *What if I choose the wrong thing? What if I would like the other selection better?* This mindset impedes progress. Historically, high-end customers are far more demanding because they are accustomed to very fine things and have unlimited resources and schedules; it is much harder to build higher-end houses. The challenging spirit of this clientele was one more hurdle I was not anticipating.

There were other issues, too. My comments are not meant to be derogatory, just truth. David's giftedness was on the field, not in the office. Mine was just the opposite. We had to reach an agreement and stay in our respective positions. There were times when we both crossed over to areas where we should not have been. I was just as guilty as he was. One day we had a sit-down heart-to-heart and pledged to stay in our areas where we could provide the most value. It was quite funny, looking back. Why couldn't we just do what we do best? Staying in your area of expertise is a valuable lesson for all entrepreneurs. You weren't designed to do everything. Select your weapon and stay on task. We all could be so much better if we would just hone our skills and stop dabbling in everything.

There was also an age difference. David is ten years older than me, so naturally he views some things differently. I'm aggressive and David is very conservative, which led to a dynamic of underlying tension.

You have to be careful about partnerships. David, as I have already stated, is a salt-of-the-earth guy. I love him unconditionally, and we would do anything for each other, even still. I'm trying to impress upon you the actual dynamics of partnerships, not trying to be critical or condescending. I am simply shooting a flare, a warning shot. I want you to pay attention to business partnerships. When you're running a business and you're looking at it from a different perspective or your tolerance for risk is different, it presents a whole set of new problems. I knew better than to get involved in an occupation that was outside my genuine interest and skills. I had gotten lazy because I'd been out of the workplace for five years. I should have taken the time to dig in and say, "We need to work through these partnership arrangements before doing this venture," but we just did not do that enough. Learn from my mistakes and always do your due diligence when even contemplating going into business with someone.

The real problem for me was working in an industry where there is limited control over subcontractors and the weather. I could control what we did; I just had no control over others or the weather. These two elements were always a challenge. The varying partner differences are no reflection on David or me—neither was right or wrong. I just didn't think through all the variables.

To say the construction business is competitive is a gross understatement. It is cutthroat, aggressive, and tough. Once I got into it, I learned pretty quickly who the general contractors were that were trustworthy and those who were going to undermine you. Along the way, a group of us got together who were honorable men and great general contractors, and we decided to form an alliance.

We created the Master Custom Builder Council, an invitation-only group; we invited only ten or twelve men of character who were general contractors to join. We formed the organization to come together to share ideas and resources, and we had regularly scheduled meetings in Nashville. A group such as this was a foreign concept, especially in custom building. When we first formed the group, I'll admit it was a bit awkward. We competed against each other daily, so to develop a group of allies seemed strange. We decided to do a parade of homes annually and give the money we raised to charity. Every year, we would all build homes for the parade of homes and sell tickets; we raised thousands of dollars. The parade of homes created a sort of showroom for each of us, and we were able to sell more houses as a result of doing that.

So what we came to realize pretty quickly was that when you form an alliance, and everyone pools resources, sharing documents, vendors, and skills sets, it's kind of like a mastermind. And guess what? There's plenty of business to go around. We weren't operating out of a limited pool because Nashville is a growing area. The last year I was in the construction industry, those twelve builders did $110 million dollars in gross sales. When you have that kind of volume, vendors want to do business with you, so they compete for the contracts. We would have three vendors per category who came monthly and pitched their product; they would give us special deals and discounts if we would give all the business to them. It made us more competitive, which gave us an edge to get more business. My point in telling you this is to demonstrate you can make adversaries into allies by pooling your resources, your wisdom, and your experience. Start working together, rather than working against each other.

> **...you can make adversaries into allies by pooling your resources, your wisdom, and your experience.**

Two are better than one because they have a good reward for their toil.—Ecclesiastes 4:9 (ESV)

There was also a sense of accountability. Builders had to reach certain standards and requirements and financial criteria before they could be in the group, so consumers knew if they were picking somebody from this council of builders, the builder had already been checked out. It turned very competitive home builders into a very positive alliance and created a home-building mecca, with fantastic credentials.

This posture can be true in any industry, whether it's coaching, construction, or retail; it doesn't matter what industry you're in, whether it's a service or if you're selling widgets. Whatever it is, your mindset has got to be to give, help, and support. When we built our parade of homes, other builders from all over the county would come in and ask questions of us. Our first inclination when they asked us a question was to hold our cards close to our vests. They would ask things like, "Where did you get that type of wood?" Or, "Where did you get this kind of faux finish?" Our natural mindset is not to share with the competition, but you have to change that into a helping mentality. We not only gave them the company, but the contact person, his phone number, and email address, and we even offered to make an introduction for them. This type of behavior creates an air of fellowship and friendship. Before you know it, everyone is winning at a higher level.

It's a mindset shift to say the more you give, the more you help, the more you encourage, the more you empower, the more you will see the natural reciprocity come back to you. Now, let's be adults about it. Some people will take advantage of this generosity. You've just got to know that up front; it's like the rotten fruit at the grocery store. You're going to throw a certain amount of it away. That's just the way it is, and you have to know that going in. But I have learned through this process, the more you can share, the more you can give, the more you can help others to connect, the better your life will be as an individual, and it's going to make your business much better in the process. Just remember to work out of an abundance mentality because there is enough for everyone! What I learned is to be wise as a serpent and harmless as a dove. You have to pay attention because I didn't say check your brain at the door.

Let each of you look not only to his interests but also to the interests of others.—Philippians 2:4 (ESV)

One tiny nugget here, and please don't miss this. People only remember what's in their favor, and it's true in most industries. No matter what business you are in, detail is essential. I learned you always need to write it down. When the detail or specification is in their favor, they never forget it, but when it's in your favor, they never remember it.

When you are building a multimillion-dollar house, there are so many details. I started doing Excel spreadsheets, with every detail to every room written down clearly. Change orders were done and signed off on and paid in advance. I didn't do that early on, and it cost us a lot of money because people would say, "I thought we were going to do this or that." No matter how honest a person someone was, everything had to be clearly written down. It's impossible for anyone to remember all the intricate details of any project. For the benefit of both parties, write it down.

In business, you're going to get an education one way or the other. You're going to pay for it through mistakes, or you're going to pay for it through education on the front end. I got an excellent education in not writing down the details. This should be done in every industry. I try to write down everything that could happen and then ask myself, *What are the possibilities? And what are we going to do if this or that scenario pans out?*

I hired my daughters to work for me, and they had to read and sign an employee contract. That way, there's no dispute. We all know exactly what we are dealing with for them and me. We go into things with a great heart, but often things don't work out the way we want. Unfortunately, 55 percent of marriages end in divorce. None of them started out with the idea of divorce. It's the same way with business deals. Everything's a great deal on day one, but there are things that need to be clearly articulated, paid attention to, and written down.

While the fastest way to communicate is to talk, the clearest way is to write it out. You intentionally have to focus on each word that's written down. It causes you to think about the ramifications of words, so you're much more likely to use proper phrasing and terms. It allows you to be clearer in your thoughts as you communicate as well.

My sister, Julie, worked for a Japanese company for years. They would go in the conference room and plan out every detail in writing. Then the next day they would go back and write out contingency plans in case the first ideas didn't work. The third day they would go back and make contingency plans for the contingency plans. They thought through situations very clearly, but once they pulled the trigger, they knew they were ready to go. They had a well-written plan at least three levels down. We should take a lesson from that culture. We need to learn to be more articulate in what we are doing; that way, there can be no miscommunication.

As we moved forward with the construction company, we floundered around for a little while, figuring out each person's role and honing in on the details. It was an expensive lesson to learn, and we knew we needed laser focus. We had to figure out the process, so we invested heavily in systems and software. Once we identified our roles completely, my partner stayed in the field; I remained in the office.

The lifeblood of a prosperous company is systematizing everything. There were changeorders implemented, processes and systems put in place, and a checklist for the checklist. Everything was documented, and we became extremely focused. It is amazing what can happen when you focus and find your niche and do what you are best at in the workplace. We discovered we weren't all things to all people. When you're speaking to everyone, you're speaking to no one. So we had to identify the exact specifics of what our general contracting role was going to be. We weren't the builder to build a $125,000 house; we didn't build decks; we weren't bathroom remodelers; we didn't redo kitchens. We did try to do these things early on, and it got us in trouble because we were trying to manage high-end residences, and on the other side of town, we were building a deck. You just can't divide your focus into two places and be all things to all people, so we chose the range of houses we were going to build, and that's what we stuck to and became superb at. Once we did that, we knew exactly who our avatar was. We knew exactly how to reach our target market and where to go to find them. We knew how to talk to them. The sales pitch for a deck versus a high-end residence is very different. I didn't have the time or the skill set to be that diverse.

> **When you're speaking to everyone, you're speaking to no one.**

In any business, you've got to identify regularly what target market you are looking for. Businesspeople building million-dollar houses are usually executives or small business owners. We identified marketing strategies to reach that person. Whatever industry you're in, you've got to narrow in, focus, and look for your exact person, your avatar. Focus allows you to define and find where your strengths are; niching down is so important because, for some reason, we always want to be all things to all people, and that is just not possible.

Let your eyes look directly forward, and your gaze be straight before you.—Proverbs 4:25 (ESV)

In my current business, as an executive coach, I have identified businessmen between the ages of twenty-eight and fifty-five as my ideal target. I'm qualified to mentor/coach outside of these specified areas, but that's my sweet spot. I know exactly what they're looking for, and I know how to help them most. I need to keep this person in mind when marketing. If you exert extreme amounts of energy in one direction, with focused intensity, you will reap great rewards.

If you exert extreme amounts of energy in one direction, with focused intensity, you will reap great rewards.

When you can tailor what you are doing to a particular audience, you will become more effective and far more profitable in the areas you are good at and want to work in. Clarity and focus will always bring greater success.

LEAN IN . . .

- When you focus all your efforts in a concentrated fashion with a well-thought-out plan, success happens.

- Always do your due diligence when even contemplating going into business with someone.

- While the fastest way to communicate is to talk, the clearest way is to write it out.

- Our natural mindset is not to share with the competition, but you have to change that into a helping mentality. Before you know it, everyone is winning at a higher level.

- Focus allows you to define and find where your strengths are; niching down is so important because, for some reason, we always want to be all things to all people, and that is just not possible.

CHAPTER 10

CHOOSE WISELY

A vi, an elderly gentleman from Israel, gave me a word of caution that I will never forget. One afternoon years ago, he stopped by my office for a visit. I was ranting about a situation that I was disturbed about. Avi asked if he might interject an opinion and told me to take a look outside. I walked over to the door and looked. He said, "You know why trees live to be hundreds of years old? Because they are flexible. When the gale-force winds blow, they bend. No matter the direction of the wind, they flex. If they were rigid, they would snap. That's why they live to be hundreds of years old." He then turned and walked away.

I have not always chosen wisely. I have been rigid to a fault, and my flexibility has been minimal. Growing older has taught me the value of patience and understanding. If I had just taken my time and not been in such a rush, I would have made a better decision about selecting a profession that matched my skill set. I came to realize that my strengths were just not being utilized as I wanted in the construction industry. It took me quite a few years to fully comprehend my wrong decision. I was sitting at my desk one Monday morning thinking, *I'm approaching fifty years old, and I'm not certain what the golden years are going to look like for me.* It occurred to me that I didn't own my business. Instead, I had a high-paying job. What I was doing in construction was trading time for money. I knew this was not sustainable. There's no recurring revenue or residual income. As long as I remained in this business, I would always be trading time for money.

I decided I couldn't continue to invest in a job. At some point years later, I would turn out the lights, lock the door, and walk away for the last time, having created nothing more than an average income. There wasn't anything to sell. We weren't building inventory. There was nothing but a name, and with our clients, it was one and done. With a fee-based company, I would be forced to wash, rinse, and repeat. It just made zero sense to me to invest a lifetime into a job, rather than a business. Businesses make money while you're sleeping. I knew there was going to be a day when I physically wouldn't be able to do this. I just didn't want to continue pouring myself into something where there was going to be nothing to sell in the end. That was part of the due diligence I didn't think through in the early stages of this partnership. Historically, I built things to sell, and there was nothing here that I was going to be able to sell as a viable business in the future. David and I were the brand.

When you're trading your time for money, you just have a job. You can say, "I own a business," but all you do is work for yourself. You just have a job, and if it costs you money to not be there, you're just selling time. I want to be able to go on vacation, and when I come back, I want to have more money, not less. That's a good business. You have to figure out a way to scale what you're doing so it doesn't require 100 percent of your time. We did that for years in brick and mortar. We had managers who ran our stores, and it didn't require my time or my being there each and every day. You can spend an hour doing something, or you can spend ten hours doing something that will return one thousand times.

How did I figure out that I wanted to be done with the construction business? It was a process for me. I would come home complaining to Robin each and every day. She would ask me what I wanted to do. I just wasn't sure. I knew we had built this business, and it was successful, and I had an excellent partner in David. We were making money; we had a brand and a following; but it was just a job. That haunted me day in and day out.

I came home one day, and I was sitting on the couch. I was frustrated because we had a client who didn't want to pay. We had just finished a big house—it was bumping up close to two million dollars. There was a seventy thousand dollar discrepancy, partially my error. I felt I was totally clear with him on the details. Remember how important I told you details were? He said he just wasn't going to pay us. He said I didn't understand what he wanted, and it wasn't fair to make him pay for that. There was fault on both sides. There were things we could have done better. It was very frustrating to have done all that work and then have him not pay. At the same time, there was a smaller project we were working on, and the same thing happened—another misunderstanding. It was one of those "I'm not sure what you heard, but I know what I said" moments. When the situation was against clients, they didn't want to do it, but when it was for them, they wanted to bleed you dry for every penny. I was so tired of dealing with that over and over.

As we were sitting on that couch, Robin looked at me over her glasses, and she said, "It's time." It made me so mad, so I just sat there and didn't say anything else. But I got up the next day and called David and told him I needed to talk with him. We met in the conference room, and I said I had to go. It was very emotional for both of us because we were friends and partners. He, more than anyone, understood my frustration because he was equally frustrated. We sat there for hours and talked through it and agreed it was time for us to part ways. We knew it was best for both of us, but we knew it would be a strain on the business for a period, so we decided to start looking for someone to take my place.

About three o'clock that afternoon, I called Robin and asked if she had any coffee made. She did, so I told her I was coming home. Keep in mind, I never went home during the day, ever. I walked in and hugged her, and while I was hugging her, she said, "You quit." I started laughing and said, "How did you know?" We sat there and reminisced over the business and talked about it and about what was ahead for us. We agreed that I would retire; I had just turned fifty years old.

...attempt to extract every ounce of value out of every situation

I do not want to discount completely my experiences with the construction industry. I formed valuable insights and relationships. Craftsmen, vendors, and clients alike taught me valuable lessons. For these experiences, I will be eternally grateful. I attempt to extract every ounce of value out of every situation. Evaluating experiences during this time revealed one crucial trait I was failing miserably at during my profession: confidence—and not the lack of it. Being in sales for my entire career gave me an abundance of confidence, borderline arrogance. One of the best lessons I learned through working in the construction business was how to express myself differently. It wasn't really about what I knew. It was how I was showing it, and I was presenting things in too straightforward of a manner.

When I'm evaluating any professional, I'm looking for confidence. If someone appears unknowledgeable, I began to question his abilities. During an interview process with anyone that I'm attempting to hire for services, if I suspect an incompetence, I'm immediately apprehensive. When entering the construction industry, I was a bit green with the processes and extremely unfamiliar with all the particulars. To compensate for my inadequacies, I overcommunicated my abilities and appeared arrogant to a few of our prospective clients. Attempting to be sensitive, which I'm not good at, I listened patiently to the criticism.

As a side note, if you hear consistent themes about your behavior, you might want to pay attention. Take heed of my advice. I enlisted the help of a competent coach who helped me to understand the value of demonstrating confidence void of arrogance. This is a much-needed skill that we could all benefit from. I'm bringing this up to say that, through this part of my life, everybody else wasn't at fault. I was to blame. I had to learn to grow through that process, and I did learn to portray my confidence with a much-needed twist called humility.

When pride comes, then comes disgrace, but with humility comes wisdom.—Proverbs 11:2

Always be in a state of personal assessment. We never get to a point where we know everything, and sometimes we learn through adversities. Often, when we're going through a trial, we need to evaluate, not just the other side, but ourselves. Ask peers and colleagues if they see where you've been in error. Ask them, "Do you see where I could have done this differently? Do you see where I could avoid an issue next time with the implementation of this policy or procedure? Do you see me as being arrogant? Do you see me being cocky?" We've got to stay in a posture of growth all the time, no matter what age we are, no matter what experiences we have had. I would even go as far as inviting constructive criticism in my life from trusted advisors.

When I retired from the construction industry, it was like an anvil was taken off both my shoulders and Robin's. There was this heaviness I had been carrying around for quite some time. We decided that day that happiness was far more important than revenue, and we chose to be happy. Happiness is not a trait; it's a choice. I'm thankful that I had other income, and I wasn't dependent on that company for survival. This is yet another reason multiple streams of revenue are not a bad idea. My passive income allowed me to be proactive in my decision. I had made long-term investing a priority earlier, and now it provided a safeguard. I would strongly suggest that you make strides in preparing for the future.

I tried every way I knew to make this occupation work, to no avail; it just didn't fit my personality. I didn't want to continue being a burden to Robin when I was coming home each day aggravated. I was setting a precedent with my negative attitude, and it wasn't healthy for the well-being of my family. My unhappiness was affecting everyone around me, including Robin, my children, grandchildren, friends, and countless other relationships. I wasn't a fun and loving guy to be around because I was irritated and unfulfilled. I wasn't operating in my area of giftedness; instead, I was in a profession that I was not enjoying, and it was affecting every area of my life. All that I have read suggests it is more damaging to you and your loved ones to be engaged in an unhealthy work environment than it is to be unemployed. If you are unhappy, change careers. I would encourage you to think through this process because you don't want to be in a situation where you have to be at a job strictly for the money. You don't want to be in a position that you have to stay at even though you don't enjoy it.

The majority of this was no one's fault but my own. I would encourage you to walk through all your major decisions with extreme caution. I rushed into this venture quickly, and I didn't have the proper mindset at the time. Consider hiring a professional who might offer insights and options. It is far better to be patient than over zealous. We pushed through and did well, but it was a constant struggle. Looking back, I should have chosen more wisely. Now, it was time to move on . . . again.

LEAN IN . . .

- When you're trading your time for money, you just have a job.

- You have to figure out a way to scale what you're doing so it doesn't require 100 percent of your time.

- If you hear consistent themes about your behavior, you might want to pay attention.

- Always be in a state of personal assessment. We never get to a point where we know everything, and sometimes we learn through adversities.

- Invite constructive criticism from trusted advisors.

- Don't set a precedent with a negative attitude because it's not healthy for the well-being of your family.

- Walk through all your major decisions with extreme caution. Rushing into a venture quickly, without the proper mindset can lead to bad choices.

CHAPTER 11

RETIRE! WHAT IS THAT?

S o here we go again: I'm retired at fifty. I told Robin it was for good this time. I told her I was completely done; I was finished; I was hanging it up. We were going to travel, enjoy our life, and just spend time with our girls and the grandkids.

This sounded good on paper, but the reality of it would not pan out as planned. I had been down this path twice previously. Robin and I spent countless hours discussing what the possibilities were for the future. We kicked dozens of ideas around, none sounding too appealing. There was a restlessness in me that's hard to describe. Was I truly finished? I had technically worked my allotted time, but was this all there was? I began to reminisce; I had had quite a bit of business experience, and Robin and I had celebrated thirty years of marriage at this time. Had God been preparing me for something larger than myself?

A Wednesday morning rolled around, and there I sat, unemployed, face to face with my mastermind group. Dan Miller flung a hand grenade into my lap. "What are you going to do now?" he asked. "I don't know" was never a right answer in that group, but I didn't know. Dan suggested, with all my experience, life and business coaching would be an excellent choice. I wrestled with that for a period of time and started thinking about what I had to offer. I've had no health issues, and physically, I'm in great shape. I take no medication, and I was in the prime of my life. I felt like I might be missing out in regards to making a difference in other people's lives if I didn't at least consider his suggestion. I wondered if I could keep some other guys from making some of the mistakes I had made. For this reason, I considered coaching might be a good option.

Now the reflection period came. When you are in this situation, where there are choices, you begin to question everything. I typically revert back to past experiences and what has worked well for me in the past. Senior adults have always been a staple in my life. I thoroughly enjoy their company, primarily because they will tell you the truth no matter what. They have nothing to prove to anyone; they are who they are with no one to

> I felt like I might be missing out in regards to making a difference in other people's lives.

impress. I love that attitude: just give it to me straight. Robin and I taught a Sunday school class of senior adults, and we loved it. It was absolutely a joy to us. We would have them over to our house for dinner. They were so genuine, and I loved being around them. They taught you the truth, even when you might disagree. As I was going through this process, I was thinking, *I'm becoming that senior adult—I'm that guy now!* Seniors have no facade. There's no pretense about them; they just tell you straight up what they think. That's who I was becoming. I thought about all the failures and successes I'd experienced over my life. I didn't want any of that stuff to be wasted.

Older people are wise, and long life brings understanding.—
Job 12:12 (EXB)

I wondered if I could help other people dodge some of the issues I had experienced. It's funny because most people don't want to talk about their failures, but everybody wants to talk about their successes. I wanted to be transparent and do both. I had been building and selling businesses for over thirty years, not realizing all along the way that I was gathering unbelievable wisdom. What if that knowledge could help other entrepreneurs to be more fruitful and significant along their journeys?

The problems don't resonate with you when you're in the midst of them. You don't understand the failures and how they will play out. You don't understand all of the successes either. Failures and success all come to a culmination at some point, when you start looking back over your life, thinking about the things you have experienced all along the way. All of these scenarios were going through my mind at warp speed.

The business experiences were countless and, coupled with well over three decades of marriage, positioned me well for life and business coaching. I have two grown daughters, Brooke and Hollie, and they are successful in their own right. Let's add five grandchildren to the mix, and now we have a full house. With all these life experiences, maybe, just maybe, I could be of help to someone. I have run up against many situations in life; maybe I could afford someone a chance to dodge an oncoming train.

The thought process of the majority of people before retiring is usually about stopping or finishing. They are just excited about being done. That is one of the main topics of this whole book. I want people to realize that living life is a process; it's not about starting and finishing and being complete. It's about transitioning and pivoting and going to the next place in your life.

It took me three times to realize that it's not about quitting. It's about living, and it's about having that view from the top continuously, the one we all are striving for. It's about looking for the next new opportunity. It's not about taking a break; instead, it's about how I can maximize my life. Honestly, I like taking breaks, but I also love looking for that next adventurous opportunity. There was a point in my life when the main thought was to get enough money so I could quit. Then the next time, I'll get just a little more money so that we'll be able to travel further and buy that next new toy. I'm terribly embarrassed to admit that 95 percent of my focus was on Robin and me. Then, this final time, I had convinced myself that I was done forever. I was not going to do anything. I was going to get up and do what I wanted each and every day. Fatigue played a big part in these decisions. Since I'm a hard charger and struggle with balance, I had worn myself out striving for the top. Each and every time, however, the pinnacle did not measure up to my expectations. So, here I was in yet another transitional period.

Two men who had been instrumental in my life for a long time, Dan Miller and Dave Ramsey, both helped me to move forward. Dan invited me to his coaching program called Innovate. I asked him what it was all about, and he told me it was where he taught people how to be coaches. Well, I was thinking about what I wanted to do with my life moving forward, but I was questioning whether I would be any good at something like this. He told me that, without question, I would be.

I'll never forget the look on his face when he talked to me about it. He said, "Are you kidding me?!" Those were his words. He said, "The experiences you have had—you've been through trials and difficult times. You and Robin have been able to weather the storms. You've started businesses; you've bought and sold them." He reminded me of all the incredible experience I could offer people and told me I was a natural for being a coach. I reminded him that I didn't go to college. He said, "Do you know how many people have asked me for my degree?" I said, "No, I have no idea." He said, "Zero! Not one person has ever asked me for any credentials. What they're interested in is your experience and wisdom, and you have an abundance of that."

I thought about it and then went home and talked to Robin; she encouraged me to attend Innovate, so I gave it a shot. I was extremely apprehensive at first, but the more Dan talked, the more interested I was.

During the event, they have breakout sessions. During those times, I had a table with about six people at it. Some of them were there with their wives, and some were alone. Dan gave discussion topics to each table and suggested we dive deep into them. When it was my turn to talk, I felt at ease. I would share my sentiments on the question and then the next question would come around. While I didn't have every answer to every question, the majority of them were pretty straightforward and simple because I had experienced them firsthand.

James, a young man at my table, asked me a couple of questions. He said, "What is one thing you would guard at all cost?" Some ideas came to mind. I said, "My heart, integrity, character, and family, without these basic principles covered, nothing else really matters." Hours went by in these breakout sessions. It was the second or third day when I got a text from Dan on my way home. He said, "Man, did you see those people at your table?" I asked him what he was referring to. He explained that they were leaning in when I was talking; he said he had watched them. I told him I was just a good storyteller. He, in turn, told me I had so much to offer and that I had to coach. That encouraged me. I showed Robin the text, and she smiled and agreed with him.

I finished up that event, and a couple of weeks later, I went and talked to Dave Ramsey. He said, "Why don't you go through our EntreLeadership Master Series? It's a pretty pricey conference, but I'll gift it to you." And I thought, *Sure, I'll do it. That's a ten thousand dollar gift; who wouldn't do that?* Dave has always been generous to the Eagles. I can't count the ways that he helps others. I would have gladly paid, but hey, why take away his willingness to bless others?

It was an excellent event, and I enjoyed the first day. I went back the second day, and everything Dave was saying resonated with me. We had been doing life together for almost twenty years by this point, and I knew most of what he was teaching. I had heard a lot of it in our mastermind group. As I was listening, I felt like what he was saying was just common sense, but then I realized a lot of people don't know this information. What is ordinary for you could be extraordinary for others.

The same thing that happened at Dan's event happened at Dave's. We would have sessions where the attendees would talk together. A couple of guys, Bret Barnhart, the founder of Barnhart Excavating in Glenpool, Oklahoma, and Matt Miller, president of School Spirit Vending, hung out with me during breaks. Both of them approached me about helping them go to the next level professionally and personally. Bret even mentioned a long-term relationship as his mentor. He said, "You will always be twenty-five years my senior."

It felt a little strange because I was at Dave's event and people were asking me to coach them. After the event, I went to Dave's office and told him what was going on and that a few guys were talking to me about being their mentor or coach. I didn't want to encroach on his generosity. He appreciated me letting him know. One of the guys called me when he got back home to Texas and asked if he could come to Nashville and talk to me about the next steps in coaching.

At this time, I hadn't even formalized being a coach. So, I went home and spoke with Robin again and told her I felt I was being led to do this. I explained that there were people already wanting me to coach them. And then Chris Johnson from Rapid City, South Dakota, called me and said he was ready for me to coach him, as well. Wow, this started happening pretty fast, right out of the gate. Officially, Chris Johnson was my first client, then Bret and Matt.

Behold, I will do something new; now it will spring forth; Will you not be aware of it? I will even make a roadway in the wilderness, rivers in the desert.—Isaiah 43:19 (NASB)

Things were just falling into place, and I told Robin I felt God was pointing us in this direction. I was getting confirmation from everyone. I had also talked to some guys in my mastermind group, and they all agreed that with the experience I had, it would be a good fit.

Dan invited me to attend additional conferences and encouraged me to come back and sit in on several other of his live events. He continued to introduce me to some potential clients, and then one thing just morphed into another. I made this decision top priority, prayed relentlessly along with Robin, and soon View from the Top was formed.

While on the surface it would appear that all of these things that happened were coincidence, I just don't believe in coincidence. The pieces for this to happen were put into place at a particular time; for me, it was at the moment I needed them. A lot of people who do not have faith consider things to be something like the alignment of the stars or just the way it is, but I believe that all good things are given by God, and I believe that there's a much bigger plan in store for our lives.

> ## While on the surface it would appear that all of these things that happened were coincidence, I just don't believe in coincidence.

For I know the plans I have for you, declares the LORD, plans to prosper you and not to harm you, plans to give you hope and future.—Jeremiah 29:11

God orchestrates things if we are willing to submit our lives to Him. We don't always understand the big picture. God doesn't waste anything in our life, including failures. He uses our successes to inspire other people.

We have to keep a humble attitude towards that and know where gifts come from in our lives. It wasn't of your making. God allows us to participate in that success. There are too many "chance meetings" for me to think they could have been coincidental. There is just no way that I could have grown those relationships or been given those opportunities if it wasn't orchestrated by God. As I've said before, we need to work like it depends on us and trust like it depends on God.

I don't think there is any substitute for hard work. I believe that we have to strategize; we have to study; we have to apply ourselves; we have to learn; and we have to use our strategies, tactics, and techniques. I think God gives us the gift of discernment to understand where we should go next. This principle is the same in business. If we will focus on adding value rather than trying to make the sale, business will increase and customer appreciation will multiply. We have to use common sense and use the abilities and talents God has given us. Then He takes all of that and uses it first of all to glorify Himself and second to bless your family. I try to stay in a constant state or posture of submission for guidance, for direction, and for trusting Him.

God knows what's best for us; He's the creator of all. Often, we think we know what's best for us, and I went through that early on in my life. It was all about bigger, better, shinier, and more. I learned that's not always what's best for me because it took me away from the most important relationships. I was always in a posture of advancement and achievement. Possessions require a lot of my time. I never want to minimize having stuff, because I enjoy having nice things, but I don't want them owning me. I want to be able to use these gifts as a blessing. Sometimes, they can be a curse if you allow them to interfere with the important relationships.

It is a pet peeve of mine for wealthy people to say, "Money doesn't matter." I want to say, "You are a liar; it's imperative. Let's take it away from you, and we will see how important it is." I want to encourage you not to make money your primary focus; don't make it a god. Make all you can for the right reasons. I love having a little financial freedom, and I enjoy what money can do for me. Just keep it in proper perspective.

Everything we buy requires time. It took me a while, but I learned to delegate my time better. While something might be pleasurable to own and I was able to afford it, it might require too much of me. I'm now at a place that I look at possessions more in terms of the time they require rather than how much money they cost. Please be very mindful of the bigger plan.

I want you to have that view from the top, and you can do that if you'll allow yourself to go through the right process. Putting your priorities in order, allowing God to lead you, and relying on coaches and mentors will go a long way towards reaching your goals.

LEAN IN . . .

- Living life is a process; it's not about starting and finishing and being complete. It's about transitioning and pivoting and going to the next place in your life. It took me three times to realize that it's not about quitting. It's about living, and it's about having that view from the top continuously, the one we all are striving for.

- The pinnacle will usually not measure up to your expectations.

- What is ordinary for you could be extraordinary for others.

- God orchestrates things if we are willing to submit our lives to Him. We don't always understand the big picture. God doesn't waste anything in our life, including failures. He uses our successes to inspire other people.

- Be very mindful of the bigger plan.

CHAPTER 12

CAN YOU HANDLE
THE TRUTH?

There are things that are paramount to our success. When I talk about success, I don't mean just monetary wins; I'm talking about life in general. I will be the first to admit I've made horrific mistakes in my life, both personally and professionally, but then I rest in the fact that this is where grace abounds. Grace has always been welcome in my life because I need it.

But he said to me, "My grace is sufficient for you, for my power is made perfect in weakness." Therefore, I will boast all the more gladly of my weaknesses so that the power of Christ may rest upon me.—2 Corinthians 12:9 (ESV)

Some things in life truly matter, and one is your character. Even with the Eagles, when we first formed the group, one of the top requirements was that you had to be a man of character.

When I think back over my life, I've had opportunities to do deals that were a little bit gray or to say things that may have been detrimental to others. There are always occasions to look the other way. Each of us has an intuitive spirit that knows what we should do, and doing those things is being a person of character.

I know from being in the pawnshop business for almost three decades there are many opportunities daily to do things underhandedly. It was a cash business. There was even a time in my life that I took some money out of the firm not to have to pay taxes, and it always felt wrong. I went to Herb one day and told him it wasn't right for us to take cash, and I was told, "You do what you got to do, and I'll do what I got to do." Hey, fair enough, but I had to stop because it was simply stealing. I went to our bookkeeper and said, "I don't want any cash. I want every dollar reported. I want everything completely aboveboard." I look back at the mindset I had then and can't believe I allowed

We can justify things any way we want in our mind, but in reality, we know wrong is wrong.

myself to be so blatantly dishonest. We can justify things any way we want in our mind, but in reality, we know wrong is wrong.

The next day, I went back into the office, and Herb looked at me and said, "Hey, Big A, I'm with you! We're going to do this thing right; we're going to quit taking cash, and we are going to report everything. We're going to do it the right way. We are Christ followers, and we need to do the right thing, and I totally agree with you." So, we did. I can show you a graph where our business escalated at that point. You see, God is waiting in the wings for us to make the right decision. He's waiting for us to submit totally. He wants us to be that person of character. There are blessings for us that are immeasurable if we'll just do the right thing.

There are a lot of people out there who are not authentic. They do one thing in public and another in private. It's just a lie. They are living a facade. As an example, some use the business credit card for dinner when it's not business or put gas in the car on the company credit card, but it's not for business. We may pay for an expense and charge it to the business to get the tax deduction. Well, that's not being a person of character. That's not being authentic. We need to take advantage of everything the government allows, but we don't need to be dishonest. When we are dishonest and we know in our spirit that it's wrong, we are not a person of character. I think we all do things when we don't know better, but when the right way is revealed to us, we should make the right decision. That's why we need people around us to challenge us, to ask us these questions, to be genuinely authentic. There are so many things that probably would happen for our good if we just would submit to the authority of God's power and to the leadership of those who have constructed the laws we live by every day. When I lay down to go to bed at night, I want to say, "I did everything that I knew to do. I was honorable; I was credible; and I was a person of character."

Pay to all what is owed to them: taxes to whom taxes are owed, revenue to whom revenue is owed, respect to whom respect is owed, honor to whom honor is owed. Owe no one anything, except to love each other, for the one who loves another has fulfilled the law.—Romans 13:7–8 (ESV)

That wasn't always the case. Early on in my business career, I lived in the gray area. I would take these opportunities that I knew, at the end of the day, were wrong, but I would just hope that I could do it and not get caught. We've got to draw the line in the sand and say, "God, I'm going to live the life I know I'm supposed to live. I'm going to be honorable; I'm going to be trustworthy. I'm going to be authentic, regardless of what it costs me."

It's so freeing when we live like this. People think living with principles is limiting, but it's the opposite. My mom used to say to always tell the truth so you won't have to remember what you said. She was so right. It's the same way with your character. The type of character and integrity you have will always come out under pressure, and when we're squeezed, people will see what's inside. God tests us through things to see what we are made of, and it's always for our good. Satan tempts us, and it's always to tear us down.

Sometimes I'll say, "Will the real you please stand up?" There was a game show in the 50s and 60s called *To Tell the Truth*. During the show a panel of four celebrities questioned three contestants. The objective was to find out which of the three candidates had an unusual occupation or experience. The impostors were allowed to lie, but the central character was sworn "to tell the truth." After questioning, the panel attempted to identify which of the three contestants was telling the truth. The host would say, "Would the real Mr. Walker please stand up?" And only the real one would stand.

> We all have a moral compass in us, but your standards have to be based on something, and for me, it's Christ.

Well, I want to ask that of you today: Who are you? What are you made of? What kind of character do you have? What kind of integrity do you have? Will the real you please stand up? And I mean, really stand up and take a position. Don't be cocky; don't be arrogant. Be a person of character and stand up.

We all have a moral compass in us, but your standards have to be based on something, and for me, it's Christ. God gives us a guidebook called the Bible. There are sixty-six books in it to guide each and every decision. Every answer to every situation is in that book. We have to read it; we have to study it; and we have to apply it to our lives. When we do that, we have a moral foundation or compass that we can live our lives by.

Lead me in thy truth, and teach me: for thou art the God of my salvation; on thee do I wait all the day.—Psalm 25:5 (KJV)

If you don't have that moral compass, then anything goes; you have no standard. And when you don't have something to point back to to say, that's my moral compass, then you're just tossed to and fro; Whichever way the winds are blowing, you ride them because you have nothing to stand on. In contrast, a moral compass sets you up for a life of integrity and transparency, and when you're open and honest with yourself and others, it puts you where you should be. Early on, when I didn't have unbiased, trusted advisors in my life, I would rationalize everything. I could make a case for anything I wanted to do. I could justify it.

Pointing back to my mom again, she would say, "If you've got to rationalize something that much in your mind, it's probably not right." She was correct. I would try to justify what I wanted in my mind, but it wasn't truthful. That's the bottom line. I might tell a story to make it benefit me, but if there was additional information I knew would help people make a different decision, I wouldn't tell that. It wasn't a lie. Actually, yes, it was. You see, withholding information that helps others make a good decision is just as big a lie as saying something that is false. I was fortunate to get people around me who were strong personalities, full of character and integrity. These guys wanted you to do the right things from an ethical standpoint. If you couldn't handle the truth, you were in big trouble being around them.

I've invited men to be honest with me, and it hurts because other people see you differently than you see yourself. When you're alone, you think you can do this or that, but when you invite people into your life and you lay out what you are doing and where you are headed and ask for their advice, it can be hard. I have been busted on a few occasions.

We want what's best for us because we are selfish. We usually make the choice we want, rather than the best choice, because the best choice may not be beneficial to us. As a Christ follower, when you're in a marriage, you are the servant leader to your spouse. There are times you have to set yourself aside for your spouse's benefit. Likewise, when you have children, you can't always do what you want to do. When I say "servant," I don't mean to be a doormat. The role of the husband in the Bible starts with leadership, but also includes provision and protection. You have to have the mindset to be there for those you love, those God has given you. It's so easy to be selfish when it comes to family, but it is our job to be there, to lead them and direct them, and if I'm not there, I cannot do that.

If you don't know the truth, you can't get better. You can continue to live in the spot you're in, but when trusted advisors come and challenge you and give you the truth, you have to listen. It's a combination of the direction you receive from those people you trust, coupled with prayer and Scripture. When those things coincide, you know what you have to implement. If you don't know the truth and are just left to yourself, you can continue to live in a lie. I just want to know the truth so that I can be a better man.

> ...you have to give yourself totally over to the posture of surrender and teachability.

It's very freeing once you get in that place. None of us are perfect. While you'll never fully arrive at perfection, especially not on your own, you must subject yourself to this kind of mindset daily.

For me, it is a total surrender to God each and every day. It's also going to those guys you can trust. Because we are in different seasons of our lives at different times, we need guidance when we are confronted with various issues or problems. So, every day, you have to give yourself totally over to the posture of surrender and teachability. And you must be completely honest—even with yourself.

I do want to caution you, when you're being honest with people, to remember to be careful how you say things. It's not always what you say to someone but how it's said. In my community, they used to call me "Frank" because if I had something to say, I would just say it straight out. I even boasted that I would be frank with you, which surrounded me with a very arrogant air. Then I went through trials and tribulations in my life that humbled me and reduced my tendency to do that. You can say things to people in a very loving, compassionate, and caring way and have a much greater impact than when you say them so frankly you appear to be cocky. So, I would just caution you to keep that in check during this process. Remember that people who love and care for you and have your best interest at heart can be trusted.

Wounds from a sincere friend are better than many kisses from an enemy.—Proverbs 27:6 (NLT)

It is easy to have your ears tickled by a deceiver and believe the words you want to hear, versus learning the truth. In all of these, transparency is what it comes down to: being transparent with others; transparent in front of God; and really being transparent with yourself. We must pull down those facades we hide behind and reveal who we truly are because that's when we can really see everything that needs to take place for us to become the people that we need to become.

I recently formed an advisory team for View from the Top. There are seven men on this team. I jokingly said to them they had to be careful about being on this team because they are going to see me naked. They said that was a visual they didn't want. The truth is that transparency is the ultimate strength. While difficult, the returns and dividends of this are enormous because you get into a posture of honesty, and you want to do the right thing. You lay yourself out and admit to not knowing everything.

It's like you are saying, "I'm going to let you into my inner thoughts. I'm going to let you into my motivation. I'm going to let you into a place where I don't allow most people to go." We want everybody to think we have it all together. We hide our trials and struggles. We deal with this a lot in my Iron Sharpens Iron mastermind groups. I tell the new guys who come in, "The sooner you can drop the veil, the faster you're going to grow, so let's just get it out on the table now. You don't have it all together. You're not strong in every area. You reveal your strengths, and you can help each other. You show your weaknesses, and we'll help you. When we get to that, you grow so much faster. Progress comes when you can say, 'I don't know where to go; I don't know what to do; I need your help.' Or, you might say, 'These are areas that God has gifted me in, these are strengths I have, and I can help you.' This kind of vulnerability levels the playing field. It lets everybody realize you can admit, 'I'm not a home run in every area.' You are admitting your need for other people, and it humbles you."

Let me just give you a quick cautionary word here. The group has got to be the right team. Don't tell all of your stories to strangers because they haven't earned the right to hear everything. You have to be willing to invest time in getting the right people around you because, in the beginning, you don't know if they are trustworthy. You don't know if these people are going to use what you say for your benefit or your detriment. You don't immediately find out if they are going to tell the world or if they will keep it confidential. It is something that takes time.

Sometimes people think they can get into a mastermind group and just start pouring everything out, but that's not the way it works. You've got to be willing to invest for the long haul to get good people around you. Some people may not work for the group, and you may have to weed them out until you get a core pack of individuals you can trust. You don't want to hear about your troubles down at the local Dairy Queen on Friday night. So I would just say be careful and take the time it takes to get those trusted, few people who will earn the right to speak truth into your life.

Instead, by speaking the truth with love, let's grow in every way into Christ.—*Ephesians 4:15 (CEB)*

Be careful about the context in which you share. Make sure it's age appropriate; make sure it's gender appropriate. There are certain things you can share with your accountability group that you don't need to go home and share with your family. They don't have the context to help you make that decision. There's a lot of transparency that needs to take place in a gender-specific situation, so others can identify the issues and help you make your decision with clarity. So, just be sensitive with whom you share during accountability.

I have chosen to coach only men for a number of reasons. One reason is that men need men to hold them accountable for problems related only to guys. Lust of the eyes is a common hurdle. Porn addiction is rampant in this modern day society. Pride and ego have ruined many a good man. It's time we were stepping up to call men out on unhealthy living.

You have to stop lying to yourself and ask yourself the right questions.

I encourage men to build a relationship with other men who can help guide them through these devastating challenges. You can be a victor.

The biggest problem initially is evaluating your life and admitting to yourself there are areas in which you need help. You have to stop trying to protect your ego and pride. You have to stop lying to yourself and ask yourself the right questions. When you are lying to yourself, you know you are doing it. Just ask yourself, "How's that working for you?" It's usually *not* working!

This happens a lot in relationships. I see where men will think one thing, but they'll tell their wives the other—rather than being honest. When things are good, that's the time to talk about disagreements. Most people don't want to start an argument, though, so they won't talk when things are good. They will wait and bring it up in the heat of the moment, when things are already inflamed. This method just exacerbates the problem. If you go to your mate and say, "Let's do a little checkup. Let's talk through some things. I'm not upset. I'm not mad, but there are some things that bother me. Can you tell me if I'm looking at it wrong? Can you help me shed some light on this situation?"

I've done this with Robin, and I will tell you, I haven't always been a champion at this. We learn as we grow through our relationships. I'll share with her what she said and explain how I feel about it. She might clarify that she didn't mean that at all, or she might say, "I did say that to you, sorry dog, and you need to change." It could go either way, but often we make things worse in our mind than it really is. If you ask for clarity, it can help. Sometimes, our motivations are impure; they are just for selfish gain, and we lie to ourselves about that. You just need to stop and think about what your motivation is and be truthful with yourself.

We do a great disservice by allowing ourselves to believe what we know is wrong. Your life doesn't get better as a result of it, and then you consistently stay in a state of tension. You're wrestling behind the scenes with the truth, and others won't tell you the truth either because you're not willing to listen. You know there's darkness there, and you don't reveal it. When you don't reveal it, light can't shine into the room because light and darkness cannot occupy the same space.

No matter how successful you become, you are only one false step, one hidden truth, or one questionable decision from ruining everything you've built. Check in with yourself right now and make sure you are where you need to be and who you need to be. If you're not there yet, then I encourage you to pray and seek truthful answers. No matter how much it hurts, it will ultimately create the type of character you need to be truly successful.

LEAN IN . . .

- Each of us has an intuitive spirit that knows what we should do, and doing those things is being a person of character.

- If you don't know the truth, you can't get better. You can continue to live in the spot you're in, but when trusted advisors come and challenge you and give you the truth, you have to listen. It's a combination of the direction you receive from those people you trust, coupled with prayer and Scripture. When those things coincide, you know what you have to implement.

- The truth is that transparency is the ultimate strength. While difficult, the returns and dividends of this are enormous because you get into a posture of honesty, and you want to do the right thing. You lay yourself out and admit to not knowing everything.

- Often we make things worse in our mind than it reality is. If you ask for clarity, it can help.

- Sometimes, our motivations are impure; they are just for selfish gain, and we lie to ourselves about that. You just need to stop and think about what your motivation is and be truthful with yourself.

CHAPTER 13

BITTERNESS IS ITS OWN PRISON

O n the way to your view from the top many obstacles can get in your way. One very large obstacle that can completely destroy your life is bitterness. When you are bitter towards a person or circumstance, it will eat you up from the inside out. You can eliminate bitterness and learn to forgive. This was a lesson I learned the hard way.

A few decades ago I was involved in buying real estate. I had bought a condo on the south side of Nashville. It was a foreclosure, and the profit was going to be pretty sweet. I held it a couple of years to take full advantage of the capital gains tax versus ordinary income. After advertising it for a couple of months, a buyer surfaced. Oddly enough, I knew him. We were by no means friends; he was just a local businessperson who had been very successful in his career (locals would know him if I used his real name). To protect the guilty, we will call him John.

To make a really long and complicated chain of events much shorter, I will just go straight to the bottom line. He cheated me out of $40,000 using a technicality that was hidden deep in the contract, unknown to anyone but him.

At the closing he pointed his finger at me, laughed out loud, and said, "I gotcha, big boy." Not only was I extremely embarrassed and mad, but he also did it in front of three other business associates. I was livid. I had no recourse, no words, and no profit by the time we finished the closing.

He left the room laughing and applauding his own genius. In his mind he had outsmarted the room and capitalized on my oversight. I got an education that day on paying close attention to details.

I left the closing with more anger, frustration, and distrust than I had ever experienced before. I was dealing with emotions that were very complex and honestly, frightening. I wanted vengeance for the first time in my adult life. Something was welling up inside me that I could not explain or clearly articulate to anyone.

He who says he is in the light, and hates his brother, is in darkness until now. He who loves his brother abides in the light, and there is no cause for stumbling in him. But he who hates his brother is in darkness and walks in darkness, and does not know where he is going, because the darkness has blinded his eyes.—1 John 2:9–11 (NKJV)

Only time would reveal that bitterness had set in, and it was painful. Every day was clouded with thoughts of how I might get him back. I wanted him to feel the embarrassment and pain I was experiencing. Not a day went by that it didn't have a profound impact on other opportunities and many of my relationships. I became very skeptical of everyone and everything. I had developed, almost over-night, a new way of looking at everything, and I hated it. A distrust set in of others, even of people who had no knowledge of my experience with John, and this did not seem fair to them at all. Bitterness became the filter through which I viewed future business, personal relation-ships, and opportunities.

I was ensnared emotionally and mentally, and I did not know how to shake it. It was a cancer, and it was consuming me.

Looking carefully lest anyone fall short of the grace of God; lest any root of bitterness springing up cause trouble, and by this many become defiled.—Hebrews 12:15 (NKJV)

A few years later, Bob, a lifelong friend, invited me to go with him and some friends to Wyoming to hunt mule deer and antelope. It took me about a second to decide I wanted to go. Everyone was to meet at the appointed rest area at 5:30 a.m. Robin agreed to drop me off because I was riding with Bob. There was a total of sixteen men riding in four SUVs. I was pretty pumped for this much needed ten-day hunting trip. I showed up on time, kissed Robin, grabbed my suitcase and rifle and jumped out of the car. I was thinking how awesome this trip was going to be. The first person I saw was Bob. I gave him a high five and told him how excited I was to be with him and the guys on this trip.

It was a cancer, and it was consuming me.

I could not believe who I saw next . . . *Are you kidding me?* There he was. The one man on the planet that I had grown to hate—John. *You mean to tell me that I was going to be on a ten-day hunting vacation with a man who had humiliated and embarrassed me and stole $40,000 from me two years earlier?* I was at a total loss. To keep down any conflict, I sucked it up and got in the Bronco. *Oh my goodness, was this going to be a long trip?* Neither of us spoke to each other the entire ride.

I can't begin to tell you how beautiful it was on that ranch. Opening morning I was sitting on top of a hill enjoying the sunrise when one of our guys below was walking to his spot. I looked with my binoculars and again was amazed. It was none other than John.

This is the moment I realized I had a severe problem. I'm ashamed to admit this, especially in writing, but the truth is, I thought about shooting him. I seriously tried to think of a way that I could shoot him and claim that I thought it was a deer. I actually had both hands on my rifle thinking through the story line and how I was going to defend my actions.

I was rationalizing in my mind how the shooting would have been justified. He should not have taken advantage of me, and he deserved everything I was about to do. *Oh my, am I really thinking of doing this?*

I was successful, well-respected, and a chairman of the deacons at my local church, and I was really about to commit murder over a business deal gone bad? *What was I thinking?* (Just a side note, I'm an excellent shot, I could have taken him. What saved him was the orange vest he was wearing. I could not figure out how to explain how I killed a deer wearing an orange hunting vest.) I was a wreck the rest of the day—for that matter, the rest of the trip.

This is what bitterness can do to you. When left unchecked, it clouds your vision and controls your decision making. All rational, moral, and healthy thoughts left my mind that day, and I was consumed with a desire, bathed in bitterness, for ultimate revenge. This is not who I am or who Christ called me to be. This is not the man my wife married or the man my children look up to. This was a man controlled by a terrible business deal for over two years.

I was so glad ten days later when we finally were ready to leave. We were just one hour away from Nashville, when John's SUV broke down on the side of the interstate. All four trucks stopped, and one of the guys said that his universal joint had broken. At first I wanted an eighteen-wheeler to run him over. And then, privately, I prayed, *Lord, I have to give this up.* I decided at that moment, right there on the side of the interstate, to let this go.

I walked up to John, and for the first time in ten days spoke to him. I said, "I have a Blazer at home I'm not using. If someone will take me to my house, I will get it and loan it to you until yours is repaired." He looked at me as though I had just punched him in the nose and asked "Why?" I simply said, "Because you need it."

There was silence for a couple seconds, and then he accepted. No one else on the trip had any knowledge of what was going on but me and John. It was a very awkward and confusing moment, but we both knew.

Right there on the side of the interstate, I let two years of bitterness go. I had to; it was killing me. It was keeping me from living a meaningful and significant life. I was captive in my mind. I decided that bitterness was no longer going to control me. I made a choice for

> I decided that bitterness was no longer going to control me. I made a choice for freedom in spite of what was done to me.

freedom in spite of what was done to me. What I realized that day is I can't control what happens to me, but I can control how I respond. I chose that day to be happy because happiness is a choice.

Get rid of all bitterness, rage and anger, brawling and slander, along with every form of malice. Be kind and compassionate to one another, forgiving each other, just as in Christ God forgave you.—Ephesians 4:31–32

I want to help you eliminate bitterness. I want you to learn how to choose happiness and choose your response when things are done wrong to you. I hope that you learn these things quickly and not harbor the terrible feelings I stored up for over two years.

I understand that sometimes we hold onto bitter feelings for years, sometimes a good portion of our lives. Letting go of bitterness does not mean you condone what the person did to you. It does mean that you are taking steps to make your own life and heart healthy. It means you are making smart choices for yourself.

That bitterness that we hold on to for so long does not eat away at the other person proving their wrongs or proving our rights. It kills us and has the potential to damage all of our meaningful relationships. It adds a negative spirit and a cutting response to our tone, and it holds us down from accomplishing so many things.

Ready or not, let's make a choice for the better. It's time to put bitterness down and move forward. Aren't you exhausted from it anyway? It is time. You are making a choice either way, bitterness or happiness. Make the positive choice for your life.

LEAN IN . . .

- When you are bitter towards a person or circumstance, it will eat you up from the inside out. You can eliminate bitterness and learn to forgive.

- Not a day went by that bitterness didn't have a profound impact on other opportunities and many of my relationships. Bitterness became the filter through which I viewed future business, personal relationships, and opportunities.

- When left unchecked, bitterness clouds your vision and controls your decision making. All rational, moral, and healthy thoughts will leave your mind, and you can become consumed with a desire, bathed in bitterness, for ultimate revenge.

- Make a choice for freedom in spite of what was done to you.

- Letting go of bitterness does not mean you condone what the person did to you. It does mean that you are taking steps to make your own life and heart healthy. It means you are making smart choices for yourself.

- That bitterness that we hold on to for so long does not eat away at the other person proving their wrongs or proving our rights. It kills us and has the potential to damage all of our meaningful relationships.

CHAPTER 14

PUT THE BIG ROCKS IN FIRST

W hen you have thirty-eight years of entrepreneurship and almost as many years of marriage, you have a lot of life experiences. Some lessons I learned well; others, not so well. I want to pass along to you the insights I have discovered along the way. A view from the top is the goal for most everyone, but few achieve it. Why? For most, it's fear: fear of the unknown, fear of failure, and for some, fear of success. One of the largest hurdles to overcome is the fear of the unknown. What will it look like in this new position? Will I make as much money as I do now? Am I smart enough to please everyone? Do I know the right people to be effective? Will I be a good dad? Do I have all the essential ingredients to be a good mate? There is a litany of other "what ifs" and questions of, "Will I be good enough?" The list goes on and on, paralyzing you. So, many days, you find yourself in this quagmire of indecision.

In your present situation, whatever it may be—whether it's personal or professional—when it's bad, you at least know how bad. As strange as it sounds, many will stay where it's bad because at least they know what they are dealing with in that present situation. There are so many facets of fear that we face daily. Permit me to share a thought that has pushed me to new heights when confronted with fear. Challenge yourself to be afraid of missing an opportunity more than you fear failure. Then, the possibilities are endless. Take a moment and think about how much more you would attempt if you weren't so afraid.

I would like to challenge an urban myth. Here it is: everyone is talking about your failure. Guess what? They're not! Neither of us is that important or popular. No one is talking about your success or your failure. We think we're a popular topic and often the central focus of other people's conversations. The truth is, we aren't. Think about it. How often do you sit at the dinner table and talk about Billy's success or Johnny's failure? You don't, and no one is talking about yours. We are always afraid of public perception, and it holds us back. Our ego and our pride keep us at bay, and we allow that fear to get a grip on us. It's a huge hindrance to leading a life of immeasurable success and significance.

I want you to ask yourself a very important question about being afraid: Are you okay with not knowing? The truth is, by not trying, we are saying it's okay not to know what the outcome or possibilities could have been. You will have to lie in bed at night and think, *Would it have worked? If I had just been brave enough to try, maybe, just perhaps, I would have hit it out of the park. But, we just might not ever know.* I, personally, could not do this.

But, you, go ahead and stay comfortable. Stay right where you are and be average. Speaking of average, do you know that being average is just as close to the bottom as it is to the top? Stop and really think about that for a second. Taking that approach would kill me. It leaves so many unanswered questions: What if I would have tried it? Could I have been successful? Would that book I wanted to write have been on the New York Times Bestseller list? Would that business have provided valuable services for people? Would I have made a lot of money? The answer to all these questions are more than likely yes, but you will never know until you try. Stop being afraid right now!

Brooke and Hollie, my daughters, would come to me when they were growing up and tell me they weren't sure if they wanted to do a certain task or a sport because they were afraid they might not be good at it. I would tell them that failure is in not trying, not in not succeeding. This mindset gave them a different perception of fear. I suggested they at least try; otherwise, how would they ever know? If it doesn't work the way you hoped, just pivot and go the other way. It's not a failure. When attempting anything in life, we either succeed, or we learn.

> ...failure is in not trying, not in not succeeding.

Where God's love is, there is no fear, because God's perfect love takes away fear. It is his punishment that makes a person fear. So his love is not made perfect in the one who has fear.—1 John 4:18 (ERV)

I'm acutely aware of how much I have talked about my faith in this book. Sometimes I have intentionally set out to mention it, and other times it just shows up. While I hope I haven't offended you, I feel as though I would be less than honest if I straddled the fence. It's just who I am. Faith can help you overcome fear because faith is stepping out, even when you're unsure. Faith would be unnecessary if you could handle it all on your own. It's pretty easy for me to relax and know that a higher power is in control. What's best for us may not be a success, as we see it. Sometimes it's not getting the things that we might be striving for that serves us best; what may actually be the best for us are unanswered prayers. There is a slight possibility the things of this world may take us away from fundamental relationships, maybe even our spouse and children. For me, placing total faith in God to direct and guide me eliminates the majority of that pressure. I'm not certain if it's humanly possible to eradicate fear completely from our lives. As a matter of fact, I think there is a need for a healthy dose of fear of the rights things—but failure is not one of them.

Sometimes, success can be about less money, not more. I will always encourage you to do everything in your power to be financially independent because I think it is great to have money. I just want you to own the money; I don't want the money to own you. Try to have a plan of what "more" is going to do for you. More can be good; we all like to have the ability to make purchases and take trips. I would even go as far as to say that there is some measure of security in finances. However, inch by inch, our pride can sneak up on us, and then all of a sudden we become self-reliant and invincible in our minds. I'm only asking that you be careful in your pursuit of financial freedom.

I caution businesspeople that I regularly talk to and tell them they need to be careful with how they spend their time because one day, when you are successful financially, you may come home with a pocket full of money to a house full of strangers. The office doesn't have a memory, but each member of your family does. At the expense of your family, you'll be successful. You might make a lot of money, but you'll come home and not know your wife. The children are playing ball, and you don't even know what season it is. Possibly, you're the only one who can provide that touch, word of encouragement, or affirmation your child needs. There is no one who can adequately fill your shoes. There are responsibilities that you are charged with that just might get left undone if you are not paying attention. Do you know what your spouse and children want? Love! Do you know how to spell that? T-I-M-E.

Lord, remind me how brief my time on earth will be. Remind me that my days are numbered—how fleeting my life is.—Psalm 39:4 (NLT)

You've got to spend time with your wife, children, and grandchildren if you are blessed to have them. Maybe you don't have any of the persons listed above, but there are other relationships that are starving for a commonality or human connection with you. Are you making sure you are contributing at the level you know, deep inside yourself, that you should? We boast and outwardly claim we are making this huge sacrifice for our families. You think, *I'm working so that they will have more of this or that.* I'm telling you to stop trying to replace time with another toy.

The ever present work/life balance is constantly on our minds. I believe it is more of a priority management decision than a balance decision. I've decided I want to pick a few nonnegotiable goals and be totally out of balance in every other area of my life. I want to pick what matters, not what I feel others think I should do. I'm totally not interested in what society dictates as important. I'm interested in knowing my family, and knowing them well.

You need to evaluate. Ask yourself, *What is my real motivation for making money? Who is it for anyway? Is it honestly for the betterment of the family, or is it to stroke my pride and ego?* More often than not, it is to stroke our ego. It's to buy things that we don't need that will distract us from those relationships that matter. If you think you are going to find more happiness in having more tangible possessions, that will never happen because happiness is a choice, not a possession. Strive to be content in your present situation, without complacency.

I have witnessed a myriad of excuses for long hours and missed activities. Some people say they want to give money away or help people in need, and the list extends on and on for external charitable causes. My question to that is "Are you giving to that cause today?" A typical reply to me is, "If I had your means and resources, I would." Sit tight for just a second; I want to challenge this statement. Money doesn't change the heart; it magnifies what is already there. If you spend little or no time now, at a small level, why do you think you would give on a grand scale if you had more? I don't believe you would give more. Start giving today, incrementally. Donate an hour or two to the local nursing home. Buy a few meals for others anonymously. Bring an enormous smile to onlookers. Do a few random acts of kindness and give your real motives and your heart time to catch up with your plan. It is amazing what generosity does for the soul. Take a second and look at your bank statement. Where do you spend your money and on what? We can get a good look at what you value by where you spend your time and money.

If you are faithful in little things, you will be faithful in large ones. But if you are dishonest in little things, you won't be honest with greater responsibilities.—Luke 16:10 (NLT)

I was a bit of a rebel when it came to designing my life. When Robin and I were married, we wanted to create our lives intentionally. We were not concerned with how our parents or friends wanted us to live. It was our life. We elected to live proactively, not reactively. We asked ourselves, "What are the things we want to accomplish?" I believe that everything good is achieved through proper planning. When we are proactive, time is on our side. It's a substantial advantage when you are choosing your path. I encourage you to spend an inordinate amount of time diving deep into your inner desires. Consider personal assessments, a behavioral test, and go as far as interviewing those who know you best. Ask the tough questions, and don't forget that others see you differently than you see yourself.

When Robin and I sit in our sunroom and plan out how we want our life to unfold, something special happens. We are unified; well, most of the time, anyway. After all, we are different people, and we are not always going to see things the same way. Even so, we talk through our differences, sometimes for extended periods of time. We have a standing rule: if we don't both agree, we don't do it. You also can be very intentional about making life happen.

Do you have a life plan? Does that sound crazy to you? Why do we make so many well-crafted business plans, complete with contingencies, and not give a second thought to how we could better live our personal life? Do you think it's possible that you are living to work? We should be working to live a well-crafted life. Work provides a means by which we can live our life and live it to its fullest. Please, don't mistake the order. Make every effort possible to design your best life. When you are filling your calendar or schedule, be sure to put the big rocks in first.

Have you ever been at work and received that metaphorical pat on the back? Then you are the man, accepting high fives from your peers or colleagues. It feels good, doesn't it? Honestly, I'm an accolades junkie. I like it when others compliment me. I even enjoy being the center of attention sometimes. I have to be careful with this because I'm easily convinced that I'm the bomb! The reality is, we all enjoy and even need a degree of praise.

> When you are filling your calendar or schedule, be sure to put the big rocks in first.

Be mindful of where that praise is coming from, however, because you want it given sincerely and genuinely. Don't fall into that trap of believing your own press. Graciously and humbly accept praise with no fanfare. If you want to empower, encourage, and edify your loved ones, recognize their efforts. Tell them you are proud of them. Show gratitude. Just like you need the accolades, so do they!

What is it that you even want? Have you slowed down enough to take the time to discover what this life is about for you? What is the reason you were put on this planet? What skills do you have? How can you give back to the community? How can you make the lives of others around you different? How can their life be better as a result of having known you?

One of the questions I ask of guys most often is this: if there were no limitations financially or geographically, what would you do with your life tomorrow? Eight out of ten can't answer that question because they are too busy trying to make a living to pay for the things they've bought that they really can't afford to begin with. We don't slow down long enough to understand what it is we want.

Then I ask this question: What is enough? Do you even know? Most people are stuck on the fact that they just want bigger, better, and more; they can't identify what's enough.

Robin and I have set benchmarks in every area of our lives. We have predetermined what we want and what we have to eliminate to achieve our goals. If there is not some type of metric or plan, I'm not sure how you implement your goals and ideas effectively. This strategy has served us well. When the nest was empty, we sold the big house. We didn't need it any longer. When we reached a certain amount of passive income, we stopped working for a period and traveled. When stress outweighed the benefits of investments, we sold them.

Why would you not do this? *Why* is always the underlying question for us. Our stuff is a tool, not the goal. The minute our life becomes entangled or overshadowed by problems with the ownership of personal or real property, it's time to let it go. He who has the most toys does not win.

What if you did it the other way? What if you were focused on living a life within your means? What if you built a life based on the amount of money you made and you didn't mortgage your soul? Robin and I, for the most part, have been very deliberate about the things we buy. Of course, we're not perfect at it; we get tripped up just like anyone else, but we give adequate time to researching our options. Haste is not your friend. Slow down; take your time.

We do have a number. We have established a financial goal that will accomplish all that we want personally. My dad used to say, "That's not hard; you just have to know what to want." Once your priorities are established, you can figure that number out as well. As you grow older, your desires change. I think part of this is, you experience certain things, and they scratch that itch. Sometimes, though, you get something and realize it's not what you thought. You just have to experience life to understand the difference. I wish I could say I have a magic formula for you, but I don't.

You can start out small when planning intentionally. What do you want your life to look like in thirty days? What about ninety days? What about in five years? It can be done in steps, so don't overwhelm yourself with a master plan that has no wiggle room. Life is moving at warp speed, and if you etch everything in stone, you will be sorely disappointed. Be calculated and intentional, just build in places to pivot.

How do you know where to go if you don't know what you want? If you stop and think about it, you can't know where to go if you don't know what it is you want. We often put the cart before the horse. How is making your life busy making your life better? People don't look at it in that regard. They are just trying to do more to earn more money to have a better life. Then our life slips by us over time. We spend all this effort and energy making more money, and we forget to live our life. So decide what it is you want so you can make a plan on how to get there.

You're blessed when you stay on course, walking steadily on the road revealed by God. You're blessed when you follow his directions, doing your best to find him. That's right—you don't go off on your own; you walk straight along the road he set. You, God, prescribed the right way to live; now you expect us to live it. Oh, that my steps might be steady, keeping to the course you set; Then I'd never have any re-

grets in comparing my life with your counsel. I thank you for speaking straight from your heart; I learn the pattern of your righteous ways. I'm going to do what you tell me to do; don't ever walk off and leave me.—Psalm 119:1–8 (MSG)

Once you decide the life you want, it's time to live it, and that's exactly what Robin and I have done for thirty-six years. As we go along in this life, Robin and I sit down together without the influence of our family, without the influence of our peers. We know it's just the two of us. We decide what we want to do, where we want to go, where and how we want to live, and how we want to bless others.

Have you ever built a house? Did you do it without blueprints? Why do we even have plans to begin with? So that we will know what the result should look like. Just apply this same principle to your life. If we are shooting into the dark, aimlessly wandering around, the chances of hitting the target are slim.

It's time to look at your life and get a plan. Consistency and regiment have been very instrumental for me. My day starts between four and five o'clock with a cup of coffee and fifteen minutes of meditation just to get myself centered. I then read Scripture, one or two chapters out of the Bible

It's time to look at your life and get a plan.

each morning. I have a very involved prayer time for individual family members, clients, and organizations I'm involved with. This time has proven to bring great benefits. This hour of the day is nonnegotiable for me.

Redundancy is annoying but profitable. Whether it be to establish habits or procedures, practice always makes perfect. I want to be redundant on the right task, so I don't allow others to fill my calendar with a menial task that is unprofitable. Plan your day or someone else will.

Put the big rocks in first. Take a hard look at what is valuable to you. Many times throughout this book, I have shared my priorities: faith, family, relationships, and then my professional responsibilities. Just like with everything else in life, if it's important to you, you'll do it. So what is important to you?

Allen Lindsey, one of my best friends for four decades, and I were having a conversation about priorities. Allen stated that he needed to visit his grandmother soon. Allen's dad, Rudy, happened to be in the room. He decided to chime in, and he always says what's on his mind. He's one of the most respected men I know. Here's what he said: "Allen, you don't love Nana like you should. If you did, you would make visiting her a priority." The room went silent; Allen's head dropped; and quietly, he agreed. We vote with our actions, not our words.

It's not that difficult to live a very successful and significant life—if you're intentional and if you live on purpose and sit down and take the time to think through the process. Look at the end goal and back up and say, "I have to delay gratification in this area to be successful in these other areas." Have you put in the big rocks first?

LEAN IN . . .

- Challenge yourself to be afraid of missing an opportunity more than you fear failure.

- Take a moment and think about how much more you would attempt if you weren't so afraid.

- I caution businesspeople that I regularly talk to and tell them they need to be careful with how they spend their time because one day, when you are successful financially, you may come home with a pocket full of money to a house full of strangers. The office doesn't have a memory, but each member of your family does.

- If there were no limitations financially or geographically, what would you do with your life tomorrow? Eight out of ten can't answer that question because they are too busy trying to make a living to pay for the things they've bought that they really can't afford to begin with.

- Redundancy is annoying but profitable. Whether it be to establish habits or procedures, practice always makes perfect. I want to be redundant on the right task, so I don't allow others to fill my calendar with a menial task that is unprofitable. Plan your day or someone else will.

CHAPTER 15
AN INDESCRIBABLE VIEW

S uccess and significance cannot be defined universally. We're human, so we have the ability to choose what we deem to be "success" for us individually. Because of this, it's hard to put a clear definition of success or significance into words. Success can look different in different seasons of life. When you are young, it means one thing, and as you grow older, it means another.

I have shared so many personal thoughts with you throughout this book and have attempted to give context for the basis of my position and beliefs. At the end of the day, what success looks like to me may not be what it looks like to you. You have to reach some understanding as to where you stand on the value of success and decide if significance is a part of your strategy.

For me, choosing my schedule and having some measure of financial freedom was, and is to this day, important. It has been very rewarding having a flexible schedule, and I consider this almost as important as the financial gain. I love being able to say I'm going to do this or that today; it's my choice. As much as I love being in control of my schedule, I also enjoy not having to worry about the incidental expenses in my life. It feels good not to worry about paying the electric bill or how I'm going to put gas in my car. You can have the same if you set your focus on the few important tasks and eliminate all the other distractions.

An engaged family, with unified values, morals, and objectives, ranks at the top of my success meter. While I was growing up, I watched my mom and dad love us unconditionally; this certainly had a profound impact on the way I view family. I never once felt like I had to earn their love or respect. We did not have a lot materially, but we were always taken care of in an adequate fashion. My parents had a work ethic that was unquestionable, and they had no problem sharing with us the importance of pulling together and doing our part. As a child, young adult, and even today, I always felt like I was important and cherished as an individual. That's priceless.

> ...set your focus on the few important tasks and eliminate all the other distractions.

Jim Rohn has a very famous quote, which I have already stated once, but believe in enough to say it again: "We are the average of the five people we spend the most time with." In my opinion, that saying is prophetic. Investing in long-term relationships has been the foundation for everything I have accomplished. I'm afraid to think what the outcome of my life might have been without my inner circle. I have been very intentional and deliberate in selecting my friends. There rarely is a week that passes that I don't have lunch, coffee, or a lengthy phone conversation with one of my mastermind members or trusted confidants. Who do you have in this important role? The time required to search out trusted advisors will be time well spent.

Having a clear conscience is very important to me. When you examine your life and begin to be open-minded about the possibilities for growth and expansion, you fully begin to realize all the areas that need your attention. During the quest for clarity towards success, you will have many unanswered questions, just as I have experienced. Having a clear conscience has become much more of a necessity than a luxury for me. If I have to explain my way out of a situation, I probably made the wrong choice. I now lean towards more conservative routes, in which nothing could be in question. This may not be the most profitable decision financially, but I sleep well.

When you were reading that last paragraph did something pop into your head that could be questionable? Is there any area in your life that needs revisiting? Remember, it takes a lifetime to build a reputation, and only one bad decision to destroy it. I'm not perfect, far from it. Every day I have to depend on God to guide and direct me because I make mistakes. Grace abounds and covers a multitude of bad decisions. While I am ever grateful for that, I can't use grace as an excuse to continually make wrong choices. Repentance is turning from something and fleeing; it's going the other way.

Submit yourselves, then, to God. Resist the devil, and he will flee from you.—James 4:7 (BSB)

Success isn't just about financial security, positive relationships, or even having a flexible schedule. One chink in the armor can create an access point for failure. There is one area of my life that needs massive amounts of accountability, and that is physical fitness. I despise paying attention to my diet, lifting weights, and running. If it's okay to loathe something, I choose physical fitness. However, this does not give me permission to dismiss it. I only have one body, and I can't buy another one. So, I work out every week. I have a trainer who pushes me to levels of cursing (just to myself, not out loud). The bottom line is take care of yourself. There are no alternatives to healthy eating and physical exercise.

Having a plan that maps out a clear direction to your goals can make success in every area of your life easier. I love having a clear sense of direction. Without a plan, it can be challenging to know if you are heading down a path that will be beneficial and profitable to you and your family. I can't begin to tell you how many times I have second-guessed myself. It's always easier looking back when connecting the dots; you can understand the reason many ideas worked out and why others didn't. You don't have that luxury when you establish your dreams. A new venture may or may not pan out; only time will tell. Your best efforts may fail miserably, and they are sure to if you don't plan well. Dream big; plan well. This strategy is a recipe for success.

> Dream big; plan well. This strategy is a recipe for success.

For me, it is impossible to reach any level of success without understanding my faith. As a Christian, my faith is pretty obvious. I'm not attempting to keep my position private or make it public; it's just who I am. I don't like it when someone uses his faith as a sales tool, and I equally lack respect for those who hide their convictions. It seems that if you are a person of faith, whatever that looks like to you, it would be pretty difficult to make life decisions not using this as a filter. Hence, this is the very reason I explore my beliefs daily and attempt to know Christ more as the spiritual director of my life. I don't want to rely on myself because I know that I'll botch it up and make huge mistakes.

When I have the Creator at the helm, I can depend on Him because He loves me. He wants what is best for me. I want to have meaning and purpose for everything I do, and for me, Christ gives that. There was a time in my life where the money was right and the schedule was fantastic, but a lack of purpose, meaning, and significance plagued me. My success stems out of a great understanding of my faith.

Seek His will in all you do, and He will show you which path to take.—Proverbs 3:6 (NLT)

Where success can be difficult to define, a broad overview of significance is meeting the needs of others and living a life that matters. Taking our focus off of our personal wants and desires is no easy task, but placing that focus on fulfilling the needs of others will return the highest rewards. I get great pleasure in engaging with others and listening to what they want to accomplish. The keyword there is "listen." Listening is extremely different than hearing. We can hear and never listen. We can acknowledge but not care. If you want to be significant in others' lives, stop waiting for your turn to speak and listen. Often, we are so excited to share what is on our mind that we miss the other's need. I'm guilty of this with Robin sometimes. I'm so interested in sharing my perspective that I fail to hear her inner thoughts. Being significant to someone else requires being a good listener.

I'm super busy. What about you? I feel tugged on at every turn; somebody always wants me to do this or that. I mean, good grief; can a man get a break? Do you ever feel this way? Please tell me that I'm not alone. When the requests come, and they do, it's relatively easy to say, "I'm busy; wish that I could help." And sometimes, I do. I have learned over time that all my days are historically full. So, when can I fit in someone who needs my assistance? I attempt to do for a few what I wish that I could do for everyone. Helping when it's inconvenient to me is significant to others. If you are waiting to help when you are not busy, you will never get around to it. Help someone today.

When you listen to others, you hear all the ways you can offer them help or guidance. Have you ever been motivated to help for the sole purpose of gain? Guilty as charged! There is this little boy in me that is selfish. "Look out for number one," he shouts from the shadows. It's okay to be smart and to understand a certain amount of good acts deserve profitable reciprocity. However, when every waking hour or every random act of kindness is attached to return on investment, there is a problem. As a safeguard against this possibility, I go through a very deliberate process. I do things for others where there is no possible way they could ever repay me. I'm talking about small acts of kindness. I'm talking about buying dinner or coffee or maybe anonymously paying a bill or sending a small gift card. Pay attention to those around you because you have daily opportunities to positively impact the lives of so many, for only pennies a day, and those chances can be squandered easily. I want to help people now who can't repay me. I want to do it often. We often do random acts of kindness with our grandchildren so that it's a teaching moment for them. We will pick out tables anonymously and tell the waitress to bring us their check. Sometimes we will pay a utility bill for someone. They don't normally know who we are, nor do I usually want them to. We have been blessed to be a blessing to others.

I was at a local Starbucks in Hendersonville early one morning meeting a client. Attempting to order, two persons ahead of me, was a very distinguished lady asking a million questions about all the possible variations of a caramel macchiato. I was getting ill just listening to her. I'm thinking, *Good grief, this is Starbucks; their menu never changes; just order something!* She continued probing deeper and deeper. I was so frustrated by this time. I needed a cup of joe! Finally, her grande macchiato arrived; she left; and I was thankful. As the guy ahead of me was placing his order, I thought, *I have to do something to get out of this frame of mind.* I was irritable, and it was starting my day out on the wrong note. I tapped him on the shoulder and said, "Get anything you want." He said, "I fully intend to." Then I said, "What I mean is, I'm buying." He then asked me why. I told him I wanted to bless him. He explained he could afford his coffee, and then I told him the truth. I said, "You see, the lady that was just ahead of you was working on my last nerve. I wanted her just to go away so that I could get my coffee. I have learned from experience that when troubling scenarios happen, we have the ability to change our attitude. By engaging in a random act of kindness, it expunges my bitterness and ill will." The ensuing conversation between the recipient and me was nothing short of amazing. I left there much happier than when I had arrived.

A couple of weeks later, I was at the same Starbucks, and I wanted to do it again. This time, I told the guy behind me to get whatever he wanted. He asked me why I would do that. Doing things like this always stirs up a conversation. He asked me who I was, and I told him that it didn't matter, I just wanted to do something for him. I got my coffee, and as I was leaving, I heard him tell the cashier, "Hey, I got all three people behind me." Generosity is contagious.

Doing for others and random acts of kindness are great examples of leading a life of significance, but so is overdelivering. As a business guy, you sometimes think, *Give them just enough to get paid. Don't throw that in; that's less profit for you.* After all, if you scrimp enough on every client, you can save enough for that much-deserved vacation. You know at one time or the other you have had these exact thoughts. In every business that I have owned, I have been tempted to take this approach. Well, it doesn't work—at least not long-term. You will get by with this method for a while, but mark my words, the word will get out that you're cheap and don't add value. Always give more than the minimal requirements. Try to provide a service or product that will wow the audience, and then you have a business! Everybody will tell his friends and ultimately revisit or repurchase. When I have truly been on my game, I've provided above and beyond the expected requirements. It's always a sweet thing when you get more than you pay for, and I strive to be a person who gives more than what someone expects. I want to outserve and outperform the competition. I want to have raving fans who wave my banner. If you want to be significant in the lives of those around you, under promise and over deliver.

Have you ever had someone say to you, "You should give; you have plenty of money to do so." Or, "If I had the money you do, I would do all those charitable activities you are referring to, as well." I hate it when others "should" on me. I want to give because I want to, not because I should. "He's got money, so he should do this." I don't want to give for that reason. I've done that in the past, and it is not a great feeling. I want to give because my heart's desire is to help others in need. What about you? Do you feel guilty when evaluating your generosity? I give because I care about others, not because I should. Significance can be discovered on multiple layers through your generosity.

Placing your personal wants and desires aside for the benefit of others is being a person of influence and immeasurable significance. This is a tough place to get to under normal circumstances. When you love someone, whether it be your children, grandchildren, spouse or others, you attempt to set your personal desires aside for his benefit. I want to prioritize my goals with others in mind. I want to delay my gratification for the greater advancement of others. This is a difficult place to get to because you are elevating others above yourself. Getting to this level demonstrates the value you place on that relationship.

> Placing your personal wants and desires aside for the benefit of others is being a person of influence and immeasurable significance.

How far ahead can you see? We are in such a microwave society, trained to think in present terms only; it's now unnatural and uncomfortable to look too far into the future. I want to have the foresight to invest long-term so that I can potentially impact generations to come. I don't only want to think about next Friday; I want to have the vision to change my family and others for generations to come. I want the family tree to change as a direct result of having been under my leadership and influence. The goal here is not to impose my values, thoughts, or direction on you as it relates to success and significance. What I want is to get you thinking about what these attributes mean to you. The interesting thing is, you can be successful and not be significant. Or you can be significant and not be considered a success by worldly standards, but there is a relationship between success and significance.

It has become apparent to me that the more we focus on significance, the more successful we become. It's just the natural reciprocity in every area, including finances. The more your focus is outward, helping and encouraging people, the more they want to do business with you and the more they want to be around you. They want to buy your service or products. They want to send other people your way. The exact opposite is also true. Self-centeredness is the kiss of death. I would question your long-term viability with that wrong attitude.

Our mindset is the key that unlocks all doors. The more time we spend endorsing, connecting, helping, and aiding others, the more we have a giving spirit. The sooner you can genuinely develop this type of passion for those around you, the better. This mindset crosses all borders—whether in business or your personal life. At the end of my final day, when they put me down six feet under, I want people to say, "That man left a legacy of wisdom. He really searched God's heart. He lived a life that was true to himself and true to others." We have one pass-through in life; we can live it any way we choose. I choose success and significance.

LEAN IN . . .

- Having a clear conscience is very important. Grace abounds and covers a multitude of bad decisions. While I am ever grateful for that, I can't use grace as an excuse to continually make wrong choices.

- Having a plan that maps out a clear direction to your goals can make success in every area of your life easier.

- Taking our focus off of our personal wants and desires is no easy task, but placing that focus on fulfilling the needs of others will return the highest rewards. Generosity is contagious!

- Being significant to someone else requires being a good listener.

ONE LAST STORY TO LEAN IN FOR . . .

I sat at the door of Panera recently writing my blog, and as people came in the door I looked at them with a very solemn look. I didn't smile; I just looked at them. I got a solemn look back from every person that came in. Nobody waved; nobody smiled. I got the same look I gave to them. Then I changed it up. People came in, and I smiled real big; I even showed them my teeth. Guess what? They started waving and grinning at me. Relationships are about what we bring, not what we take. If you want a great life, you have to bring a great life.

NEXT STEP

Congratulations, you finished step one! The journey to your very own View from the Top has begun, but this is just the beginning to a journey of a lifetime.

Don't stop now.

Don't even pause!

Success is a team sport, and you don't have to make it on your own. I have personally put together resources that will help you. All you have to do now is follow some very simple instructions.

Step 1. Go to www.ViewFromTheTop.com/leanin right now.

Step 2. Type your First Name and your Primary Email Address in the spaces provided.

Step 3. Click the button that says "Next Step."

You will immediately be given access to the information you need to move towards your View from the Top.

That's it.

Easy, right?

You can't move forward by standing still; you must take action. Get these resources today and start building your View from the Top!

LIVING THE TRANSFORMED LIFE

I have been abundantly clear in this book that my life is wrapped around my Lord and Savior, Jesus Christ. Without Him, my life would look very different.

I wanted to share with you the Romans Road to salvation, in hopes that you might also desire a "View from the Top" with Jesus Christ by your side.

I have come that they may have life, and that they may have it more abundantly. (John 10:10b, KJV)

You must acknowledge God as the Creator of everything, accepting your humble position in God's created order and purpose.

For since the creation of the world His invisible attributes are clearly seen, being understood by the things that are made, even His eternal power and Godhead, so that they are without excuse, because, although they knew God, they did not glorify Him as God, nor were thankful, but became futile in their thoughts, and their foolish hearts were darkened. (Romans 1:20–21, ISV)

You must realize you are a sinner and in need of forgiveness. Because of sin, you are separated from God.

For all have sinned and fall short of the glory of God. (Romans 3:23, KJV)

The penalty for this sin is death.

For the wages of sin is death, but the gift of God is eternal life in Jesus Christ our Lord. (Romans 6:23, KJV)

God gave you a way to be forgiven of these sins. He extended His love by giving you the opportunity for life through the death of His Son, Jesus Christ. Jesus paid your penalty!

But God demonstrates His own love toward us, in that while we were yet sinners, Christ died for us. (Romans 5:8, NKJV)

If you repent of your sin, then confess and trust Jesus Christ as your Lord and Savior—knowing he died, was buried, and raised from the dead for you—you will be saved from this sin. Just call upon the name of the Lord, and you will be saved!

For whoever calls on the name of the Lord shall be saved. (Romans 10:13, KJV)

That if you confess with your mouth the Lord Jesus and believe in your heart that God has raised Him from the dead, you will be saved. For with the heart one believes unto righteousness, and with the mouth confession is made unto salvation. (Romans 10: 9–10, NKJV)

This Roman Road shows you the path. Are you ready to accept God's gift of salvation now? If so, believe in what Jesus Christ did for you on the cross, repent of your sins, and commit the rest of your life to Him. Below is a guideline prayer for your step of faith:

Lord Jesus,

I know that I have broken your laws and my sins have separated me from you. I am truly sorry, and now I want to turn away from my past sinful life toward you. Please forgive me, and help me to avoid sinning again. I know You have loved me so much that You were willing to submit to the cross and die on my behalf. That's a grace so amazing I cannot possibly fully comprehend it, but I do accept it. I invite you, Jesus, to become the Lord of my life, to rule and reign in my heart from this day forward. Please send your Holy Spirit to help me obey You and to do Your will for the rest of my life. I want to spend the rest of my life serving You and experiencing the joy that only You can offer. In Jesus' name I pray,

Amen.

Praying that prayer means you are now a new creation in Jesus Christ. The road ahead will be full of life-changing experiences. Growing in knowledge and understanding of the Bible and your Christian walk with God is essential for your spiritual growth. Here are some ways that you can grow as a Christian:

- Study His word, the Bible.

- Be baptized because baptism identifies you with Christ.

- Get involved with a local church.

- Find fellowship with other Christ followers.

- Make prayer an essential part of your daily life.

- Share your faith with others.

For God so loved the world that He gave His only begotten Son, that whoever believes in Him should not perish but have everlasting life. (John 3:16, KJV)

If you've said the sinner's prayer and want to know how to move forward in your Christian faith or if you would like to know more about a personal relationship with Jesus Christ, please email me at transformed@ViewFromTheTop.com.

ABOUT THE AUTHOR

A fter starting and selling a number of businesses, including one to a Fortune 500 company, Aaron decided to sit back, relax, and enjoy retirement. What he discovered was that fifty was way too young to hang it up. His retirement lasted for eight months; or until he was approached by friends and fellow mastermind members, Dan Miller and Dave Ramsey. These two men encouraged Aaron to pursue a purposeful and meaningful career as a life and business coach. Dan and Dave pointed back to Aaron's success starting and selling multiple businesses and reminded him of his marriage of over three decades, a feat enjoyed by very few couples.

Aaron realized that his true calling in life was to help men move beyond a mindset dominated by the single dimension of their careers. He helps men realize they need not choose to choose their profession over their relationships. Aaron masterfully introduces the concept of "Success & Significance" into men's lives. Aaron has developed and leads a global

community of like-minded men equally focused on the success to significance journey.

Many are familiar with Zig Ziglar's famous quote, "You can have everything in life you want, if you will just help enough other people get
what they want." Aaron lives and breathes this philosophy. His uncanny
knack to develop businesses that are centered on deep, meaningful personal relationships is rarely found in today's world. He helps the men in
his sphere of influence to understand that serving others is the greatest
calling you can have and that this calling leads to personal, professional,
and spiritual growth.

Aaron is known for his candor, compassion, and tough love. His successes, failures, and trials have uniquely equipped him to help men through
life's journey. He is just as likely to be heard telling the men he works with
"You're Awesome" as he is asking them, "What kind of a knucklehead are
you?" He's passionate about helping men understand the importance of
accountability in their lives and in their businesses. Being challenged intentionally by nonbiased peers and mentors is the bedrock of Aaron's success.
It's incumbent upon us as men to be held accountable to ourselves, our
families, and our faith.

Aaron values his time spent with family and friends above all else.
Sharing the past thirty-six years with his lovely wife, Robin, has been nothing short of spectacular. His two fantastic daughters and wonderful sons-
in-law have given Aaron and Robin five beautiful grandchildren. When
time allows, Aaron enjoys the great outdoors, not limited to but including
hunting and fishing.

Aaron has two life mantras:

Fear missing an opportunity more than you fear failure.

Can't couldn't do it, and Could did it all.

A free eBook edition is available with the purchase of this book.

To claim your free eBook edition:

1. Download the Shelfie app.
2. Write your name in upper case in the box.
3. Use the Shelfie app to submit a photo.
4. Download your eBook to any device.

Shelfie

A **free** eBook edition is available
with the purchase of this print book.

CLEARLY PRINT YOUR NAME ABOVE IN UPPER CASE

Instructions to claim your free eBook edition:
1. Download the Shelfie app for Android or iOS
2. Write your name in **UPPER CASE** above
3. Use the Shelfie app to submit a photo
4. Download your eBook to any device

Print & Digital Together Forever.

Snap a photo

Free eBook

Read anywhere

Morgan James
Speakers Group

↗ www.TheMorganJamesSpeakersGroup.com

We connect Morgan James published authors with live and online events and audiences whom will benefit from their expertise.

Morgan James makes all of our titles available
through the Library for All Charity Organization.

www.LibraryForAll.org

CPSIA information can be obtained
at www.ICGtesting.com
Printed in the USA
BVOW03*1146120617

486607BV00007BA/260/P